## Advance Praise

"**Zen Money Map** by Liz Lajoie is meaningful blend of Mind, Art, and the Soul that guides business owners in navigating their financial lives with intelligence, intention, and care. This book is a must read for entrepreneurs who are great at what they do but are not quite as comfortable with the complexities of money. Liz provides great examples, exercises, and relatable stories that are sure to inspire, influence, and support even the most fearful."

**– Michael F. Kay, CFP®**
**Author of *The Feel Rich Project* and *The Business of Life***
**www.financial-lifefocus.com**

"**Zen Money Map**, by Liz Lajoie, is so clearly written for readers with exactly the need she is highlighting: It's all about individual relationships with money, but finally in a way that ties it comfortably to business objectives, larger missions, and recognizing our own value and the value of our superpowers we are bringing to our clients. Easy to read, but filled with very practical and actionable exercises, Ms. Lajoie takes the reader on a journey that can end up in only one place: Financial Clarity and Alignment. If you are scared of, avoid, hate, are frustrated by, or otherwise have a broken relationship with the finances in your business – this is the book for you. She carefully takes you from A to Z with *careful, and bite-sized steps. I will be recommending it to my own clients; wherever I'm a CFO, this is a must read."*

– **Pam Prior**
**Author of *Your First CFO***
**www.prioritiesllc.com**

*"Once upon a time there was a new entrepreneur who didn't know what she was doing and had no concept of the money in her business. But the Universe had a budding idea to bring her the most magical Financial Fairy Godmother in the whole land. There are no words for what Liz Lajoie is capable of doing to help support and grow your business. Since working with her, my business has more than doubled its revenue, and I don't believe it would have been possible without her guiding my financial ship.*

*Reading* **Zen Money Map** *was the most beautiful marriage of financial know how, and spiritual go-get-it. Merging money beliefs into strong new foundations, this book and Liz's guidance have allowed me to take back control of my money and make powerful choices in my business. I loved this book! Period! I inhaled it in one sitting. A must read if you are serious about learning to pay yourself in your business and make a difference in the world."*

– **Tamara Arnold**
**Author of *The Magical Business Method***
**www.tamaraarnold.ca**

# Zen Money Map

# Zen
# MONEY
# MAP

*Charge Your Worth,*
*Pay Yourself First,*
*and Fund Your Wildest Dreams*

# LIZ LAJOIE

NEW YORK

LONDON • NASHVILLE • MELBOURNE • VANCOUVER

# Zen Money Map

## Charge Your Worth, Pay Yourself First, and Fund Your Wildest Dreams

© 2019 Liz Lajoie

Published in New York, New York, by Morgan James Publishing in partnership with Difference Press. Morgan James is a trademark of Morgan James, LLC.
www.MorganJamesPublishing.com

ISBN 9781642792300 paperback
ISBN 9781642792317 eBook
Library of Congress Control Number: 2018910321

**Cover & Interior Design by:**
Christopher Kirk
www.GFSstudio.com

Morgan James is a proud partner of Habitat for Humanity Peninsula and Greater Williamsburg. Partners in building since 2006.

Get involved today! Visit
MorganJamesPublishing.com/giving-back

## Dedication

*For Finn and Nia, my loving and wildly generous children. Thank you for being my guides on my path to Zen and inspiring me to look beyond the immediate horizon every day.*

# Table of Contents

*Introduction* . . . . . . . . . . . . . . . . . . . . . . . . . . . . . . . . . . . . . . . . . xi

| Chapter 1 | The *Zen Money* Journey . . . . . . . . . . . . . . . . . . 1 |
| Chapter 2 | The Right Understanding . . . . . . . . . . . . . . . 13 |
| Chapter 3 | The Right Thought . . . . . . . . . . . . . . . . . . . . . 29 |
| Chapter 4 | The Right Speech . . . . . . . . . . . . . . . . . . . . . 45 |
| Chapter 5 | The Right Action . . . . . . . . . . . . . . . . . . . . 69 |
| Chapter 6 | The Right Livelihood . . . . . . . . . . . . . . . . 89 |
| Chapter 7 | The Right Effort . . . . . . . . . . . . . . . . . . . . 103 |
| Chapter 8 | The Right Mindfulness and the Right Concentration . . . . . . . . . . . . . . . . . . . . 119 |
| Chapter 9 | The Middle Way . . . . . . . . . . . . . . . . . . . 135 |
| Chapter 10 | Your Bottom Line . . . . . . . . . . . . . . . . . . 147 |

*Further Reading* . . . . . . . . . . . . . . . . . . . . . . . . . . . . . . . . . . . . . . 151

*Acknowledgments* . . . . . . . . . . . . . . . . . . . . . . . . . . . . . . . . . . . . 153

*About the Author* . . . . . . . . . . . . . . . . . . . . . . . . . . . . . . . . . . . . 155

*Thank You* . . . . . . . . . . . . . . . . . . . . . . . . . . . . . . . . . . . . . . . . . . 157

# Introduction

I have a confession to make. I've been making a habit of talking about money and emotional well-being in the same breath. It hasn't been on purpose, and it's kind of taken me by surprise, if I'm honest. Because as a straight-up small business management person, my entrepreneurial background has been pretty black and white for the past 15 years or so. Except conversations – about feeling good in terms of your money situation, developing financial flow, and mindset shifts – keep happening. Partly because I work with a lot of spiritual and creative entrepreneurs who talk in less business-y language and I always try to meet people where they are. Partly because I've come to see the emotional scars we all carry when it comes to money and how important it is to work on healing them alongside learning financial how-tos. And partly because my own journey has included tapping into something bigger than myself.

So, this conversation about how to make peace with our internal money turmoil is really a natural extension of my work as CFO and financial teacher to online entrepreneurs.

And when I question whether I'm the person to talk about the emotional side of finances, the question "Who are you *not* to?" keeps coming to mind. Being able to help entrepreneurs heal their relationships with money and find their *Zen* through the implementation of sound financial practices is the highlight of my work. And having this conversation with you here is an honor, because I know the power of this kind of learning and recognize it's my gift to share it.

The reality is that the "money stuff" is truly difficult for many of us. Not because the concepts are particularly difficult or the practices time consuming. We're trapped by what we learned (or didn't learn) early in life, by beliefs that we're not good at it, or that it's not important, or a variety of other ideas that keep us from stepping fully into the role of "good manager of money." It holds us back from achieving our full success as entrepreneurs, can stop us from crossing from six to seven figures, and makes us sweat when we have to decide how much to pay ourselves or when we can invest in growth. It can be truly debilitating.

One of my clients can only talk money with me while she's lying down. We've tried to have video conference calls in a more formal setting and it simply doesn't work. She invariably needs to get horizontal for us to have a meaningful conversation. She feels so weighed down by the financial work she *knows* she needs to understand as a successful business owner, that she physically cannot be upright. It seems crazy, but we've just learned to go with it, because it's part of her process of becoming comfortable with her money, both within her business and in her personal life.

In sharing stories like hers, my goal is to help you let go of those internal roadblocks and find a path to *Zen Money*™

that feels easy and expansive. One that will help you lose that millstone hanging around your neck whenever you think about your finances (or that makes you need to lie down) and will free you up to feel confident and secure in your money decisions. In my work with entrepreneurs like you, I've found that talking about the *whats* and the *whys* isn't enough to help them step up as CEO of their companies and feel confident making sound financial decisions. Often, it's not the basic how-to that trips us up (although we might tell ourselves that story); the mental gymnastics around our discomfort with money are the real roadblock to finding *Zen* in our financial lives.

Putting off getting cozy with your money can cause a *lot* of stress and even physical discomfort. We want to earn a lot of money, but we also fear having it. We're concerned about "getting it wrong" or feel genuinely nauseated when the bank statement shows up. As entrepreneurs, the money discomfort is more acute because of the pressures we feel in charging our worth, figuring out how to grow our businesses, and paying ourselves so we can live the life of our dreams. We secretly think that if we just work harder, the money will follow, and we won't have to actively get comfortable with all that ourselves. It does happen that way occasionally, but if not, the uncertainty can be debilitating.

Financial upheaval is the number one reason that over half of entrepreneurs fail in the first five years in business, and the numbers are much higher in the online space. The reality is that getting a handle on our money and building a strong financial pillar often comes fairly late in the game for most of us in this space. Particularly if you're an entrepreneur who might be just a *little* bit numbers averse by nature. Or maybe you're a busy consultant who just really wants to work with clients and have someone else handle all that money stuff. There are always good reasons we haven't yet jumped into learning more about our finances.

So, why do we shy away from learning how to make our money work for us, especially when we're so invested in building a strong and meaningful business? Because it can be viscerally uncomfortable, and when we feel that way, we're ashamed because we think we *should* understand it easily. So we shy away from the topic at all costs, sometimes to very unfortunate consequences.

What if you could change that story for yourself and your business? What if you knew for certain how to make sure you have enough cash in your business to feed your personal life? Can you imagine not cringing when you consider your actual income and expenses, or not feeling buried in sand when tax time looms? In my experience, the very act of getting comfortable with financial concepts and basic practices can go a long way to healing this dis-ease around money.

And here's the cool thing: when we understand how to build a bridge between our business and our personal lives, the flow of money becomes easier and we feel more confident in our role as CEO (whether we use that title or not), and whether we're a *solo-preneur* or manage a staff of twenty. Whatever your circumstances, you're here now because, deep down and despite a little internal cringing (or a lot), you know that your financial health needs attention. That might be to continue growing your business past that initial holy grail of six figures. Maybe you're reading this book because you're tired of not knowing how much you can pay yourself out of all your hard work, or you're secretly embarrassed because colleagues or the people in your mastermind talk in a language you don't quite understand.

Whatever the case, together we're going to look at your money stories, develop easy-to-understand financial habits that will support your business growth, help you determine exactly how much you can pay yourself, and make a plan that will fund your wildest dreams … all without you wanting to throw up. I believe that connecting all the dots around money is important to not only hitting all of your big goals, but most importantly, to feeling *great* about everything that's happening with your finances in your life.

I'm convinced this conversation is acutely needed in the entrepreneurial space, given everything I've learned on my own journey in business and from my clients over the years. That includes coming face to face with the emotional, and even spiritual, resistance that has kept us from establishing a healthy relationship with our finances in the past. To be truly meaningful, our understanding of money needs to encompass all areas – not just business – and be tied to our biggest *whys*, whatever they may be. When we can clearly see how money works in our company, and how it can flow to our personal lives and support our goals, it's a wonderful thing.

This book is for entrepreneurs like you looking to understand how to use money to your best advantage, both in your business and your personal life, and as a result, redefine your relationship with it. I'd love for you to truly find your *Zen* as you continue to grow your business and create change in the world, because you have a money strategy that feels good and makes sense for *you*. That strategy is going to look different than anyone else's and should be as unique as you are. To be truly successful – in business, in life, as a human being – we need to develop a *Zen Money Map*™ that fully serves *you* and *your* goals. A cookie cutter approach will simply not do.

In the pages that follow, you'll find a combination of business financial how-to and money mindset strategies designed to help you shed your discomfort and step fully into your role as leader of your company, to understand what you need to pay attention to, and when you can ask for help. You'll build a financial plan specifically tailored to you and your goals. And most importantly, you'll learn how to leave that weight of uncertainty around your money management behind you once and for all as an entrepreneur.

Are you ready to begin? Let's dive in and start building your *Zen Money Map*!

## Chapter 1

# The *Zen Money* Journey

*"You have to take risks. We will only understand life fully when we allow the unexpected to happen."*

**– Paulo Coelho**

L ike many entrepreneurs, I've been blessed with a twisty employment road. I've worked in the non-profit sector and corporate banking; I ran away to Prague and taught English for a time; I learned how to run a medical manufacturing company; and worked my way from administrative assistant to business manager/partner in a multi-million-dollar engineering firm, among other things. Along the way, there were two constants: my personal drive and my fear around finances.

If you'd told me when I was 20 that I'd be helping entrepreneurs sort out their money game, I'd have laughed in your face. Who am I to talk about financial bliss? At that age, I had so much fear about money (how to earn it, how it works, how to use it well) that my younger self could have never imagined replacing that terror with confidence. Much less using that confidence to earn a living! It seems ironic now, given that most of my time is spent talking financial strategy with successful entrepreneurs.

And yet here I am. My first book, *From Zero to Zen,* was based on work I've done with new (and not-so-new) entrepreneurs to help them learn how to take care of their finances in order to build a successful business. The "ticky-tacky" stuff, as I like to call it. It teaches you best practices for your money management as a small business owner – what to do and when – so you can stop feeling like the other shoe is going to drop any second.

In that work, however, I realized that knowing the *whats* and the *whens* wasn't fully getting to heart of the matter for many of my clients. These are smart, capable people I'm talking about. They've jumped into the entrepreneurial waters and learned how to make a go of it. They could certainly learn what they were "supposed" to be doing, but many couldn't seem to make the new habits stick. We'd set up systems to take care of their finances, and they'd be excited for a while, but eventually (or immediately) I'd find they would revert to their status quo of not really reviewing their numbers, and not keeping their records up to date if I wasn't there to "take care of it" for them. I wondered what was going on, since my clients were dedicated to their work, making money, and consciously *wanted* to run their businesses well. They'd signed up to learn how to manage their finances in a way that felt better, and yet, here they were, relapsing to their old familiar habits of ignoring their money management, with a bonus of feeling extra guilty about it since they now "knew better."

This pattern kept repeating itself. Not with everyone, certainly, but with enough that I started having another layer of conversation with people as we worked through the day-to-day financial management process together. I became genuinely curious about what was holding them back from what I saw as an easy answer to their problem: learn to do things better and feel great in the process. Because many of my clients were resisting the heck out of the first part and were missing the last part entirely. They enjoyed working with me, but the financial tasks themselves felt overwhelming.

At that point, I realized that the type of clients I attract tend to be darn numbers averse. Sometimes technologically irritable as well. For them, the very act of learning a platform, or even using a calculator at times, was uncomfortable. They wanted to feel better about their money stuff, but they were hyper-resistant to doing the work, and many carried stories about being "bad with money" or "the worst" with math that were hanging them up. Some part inside was telling them that the new language of finance I was trying to teach was just too hard. Another part really wanted to level-up around their money, so working with me was putting them right in the middle of an internal conflict that had been brewing for years.

## Learning to Manage It All

I was befuddled for a while and frustrated that I couldn't solve this problem easily for my clients. And then I remembered how hard it had been to learn how to juggle business numbers and my own numbers. As I related in my first book, most of my financial learning as an adult happened in a short period of time. Up until my late twenties, my relationship with money was muddy. I could save when I needed to, like when I wanted to move abroad and spent a year living on ramen and never going out (much to the chagrin of my friends) so that I could pay down my credit card debt and create a financial buffer for myself. That experience felt *amazing*. Like sticking with a diet long enough to see significant results.

However, I went right back into debt once the card was cleared and when I moved back to the States in the early 2000s, I once again had the millstone of a credit card balance hanging around my neck. I use that analogy a lot in my work, because that's how our money situations can often feel. Like a weight dragging us down. Sometimes it becomes so comfortable we can't imagine a life without it as our constant companion. If you've gone through medical school in the past 20 years, you know what I'm talking about!

But you don't need an "official" reason like expensive schooling to create that feeling. Before I met my husband and began seriously learning how to manage a business successfully, money was something I desperately wanted, and yet as soon as I found it, it'd disappear faster than you can say "boo." It always seemed like there was something critical to my happiness, well-being, or success that had to be purchased. And while I enjoyed making lists (hello, Type-A numbers girl over here), and could stick to short term goals, I didn't have a clear sense of the bigger picture of money or how to use it strategically. Hand-to-mouth was my *modus operandi* and I couldn't see how to move past living that way.

Then I began my own entrepreneurial journey, and along the way I learned the bliss of having "enough," of making the sometimes-hard spending choices, and how to best handle cash flow in a business. While I was getting my MBA and being recruited into ownership at my engineering firm, I was also becoming a mother of two and learning to manage present, short-term, and long-term future financial goals without freaking out.

Don't get me wrong, my old self didn't go quietly. I remember a conversation with my husband before we were married. I'd gone out and spent several hundred dollars on new dishes. To me, this seemed a perfectly legitimate expenditure, since his dishes were all mismatched and cracked (and frankly, I wanted to bring a little bit of "me" when we moved in together). All totally legitimate. Plus, they were crazy on sale. So, I could *not* understand his absolute disgust with me. Okay, that might be a bit of an overstatement (he's not an ogre), but to him, it was a complete waste of money, being the frugal, recycling type he is. It took a while to feel comfortable looking at spending through a lens of "What is enough?" and "Do we really need that?"

It helped that my professional life was spent amidst a group of highly analytical nerdy types. I don't know if you have any engineers in your life, but they tend to be as frugal as my husband and inherently understand how to use the basic financial equation (income - expenses = profit) to their advantage. So, I learned quickly how to make a dollar stretch and to always ask "Do we really need this?" before making a spending decision. Sometimes the answer was no, and we found another way to accomplish the same goals. Sometimes the answer was yes, and we went out on a financial limb knowing exactly why we were doing it.

Given all of that happening around me, over time the art of giving our money jobs to do, with intention, and without fear, became my norm. It happened so subtly I wasn't sure I could explain it to anyone else. However, given my clients' continued discomforts as they tried to up-level their entrepreneurial game, I had to try. It became clear that the teachings in *From Zero to Zen* weren't the final answer; they instead became a great staging ground for the work of building our *Zen Money Map*.

At first, it happened organically. I felt as uncomfortable with my clients' discomfort as they did, most of the time. So, we started talking about how to use their financial tools consistently, in order to overcome their feelings of inadequacy and resistance around their finances. I kept encouraging them to just start doing the work, like their laundry. To check in with their numbers every week, even when it felt hard, because the outcome, like clean clothes, was worth the effort.

In the process, I realized that my encouragement was similar to learning I was doing myself around meditation and self-care. You have to keep showing up, even when you can't see the end game clearly. The very act clarifies the process. Like putting on goggles after swimming in murky waters. Your vision clears, and you understand *why* the repetition of your money practices is so important.

So, basically, all this was percolating in the background as I published my first book, continued the training program it's based on, and continued working with clients in the online entrepreneurial space as their CFO. And then I read *The Soul of Money* by Lynne Twist and I knew how to finally take the conversation to the next level.

## The Big "AHA"

As I said, I'd been struggling to speak clearly about the issues I saw coming up with my clients around their money management and how to help them make a meaningful transition to feeling *Zen* with their finances in both their businesses and their personal lives. I knew it was possible, but there was something missing in the work I was doing, a disconnect between the day-to-day financial work and the feeling of ease we were aspiring to achieve. And then I realized that we needed to integrate the big picture of *why* into the conversation to make it truly meaningful. My clients weren't fully stepping into their role as business owners because all the money stuff just felt like a big fat *should*. And as we all know, when we have a *should* it rarely feels good.

Which is where *The Soul of Money,* which looks deeply at our relationship with money from a spiritual and community-driven view, comes in. In it, we're asked "How can we be our best selves around money?" The author, Lynne Twist, writes:

> *"We all have an identifiable, though largely unconscious and unexamined relationship with money that shapes our experience of life, and our deepest feelings about ourselves and others. Whether you count your change in dollars, yen, rupees, or drachmas, money is the one central, linchpin issue in all our lives. Everyone is interested in money, and almost all of us feel a chronic concern, or even fear, that we will never really have enough or be able to keep enough of it. Many of us pretend that money isn't important to us or think it shouldn't be. Many live openly with the accumulation*

*of money as our primary goal. And no matter how
much money we have or don't have, the worry that
we don't have or won't have enough of it quickens our
heart around money issues. The harder we try to get
it, or even try to ignore it, or rise above it, the tighter
money's grip on us grows."*

Many, many people I know struggle with these same
discomforts, both in and out of the entrepreneurial world. The
book made me realize just how uncomfortable the relationship
with money is for so many of us, and how deeply it runs. And
I already knew that teaching people how to manage their books
and take care of their business finances was not quite enough,
because nearly all the conversations we were having were based
around deep fears of being in lack, of not being capable enough
to handle their finances, and of feeling completely lost. It was
rarely about the actual "how-to." That was simply the crucible
for this other, emotional conversation.

The more I began to talk openly about how to feel great
about your money management through the lens of the "ticky-
tacky" financial stuff, the more aspects of dis-ease around money
came up. It also became clear that talking simply within the
parameter of business was not enough. People are starving to
feel confident around their money decisions, including *all* areas
of their life. So, the conversation needed to change and expand.
In reality, I'd been having it all along with my clients anyway,
because I'm incapable of narrowing my focus to "just business."
Why? Because my clients, for the most part, *are* their businesses.
And personal financial management questions inevitably crop
up as they begin to understand their business finances.

And so the *Zen Money Map* was born, when I started coherently integrating the *why* into the work I was doing with six- and seven-figure entrepreneurs. That work proved so positive and life-changing that I felt the message needed a broader audience, which leads us to the book in your hands today. I hope you find the following chapters a doorway to a more peaceful, powerful relationship with *your* financial world.

## Zen Money Tenets: The Eight-Fold Path

I called my first book *From Zero to Zen* because of a vague idea I had that *Zen* meant easy and being at peace. I didn't have much of a background in actual *Zen* practices. But somewhere inside, I knew that the idea was the right one, so I went with it. Because, really, who doesn't want to feel *Zen* about their money? I sure do!

Since selecting that title, I've been on a spiritual journey myself. As I shared in my first book, yoga and meditation have become the cornerstones of my recovery from chronic Lyme disease. Over time, I've deepened my practices and expanded my own understanding. Not that I consider myself a Buddhist or even particularly knowledgeable. But I've been introduced to the basic tenets of *Zen* and find them beautiful. In Zen Buddhism, there's a concept of the Eight-Fold Path, which is believed to be a guide to the end of suffering.

Now, I'm not asking you to embrace a spiritual methodology here or become all woo-woo if that's not your thing. But in my work, I've come to see that our relationship with money truly is a cause of suffering for many people. And if we take the principles of these teachings and apply it to our money reality, it becomes a fantastic framework for shifting our understanding, our strategies, and our very being when it comes to our money. Much of what follows can be found in other financial how-to books, with a critical twist: just because you know *what* to do doesn't automatically mean you're doing it well (or sometimes at all). If you're like many entrepreneurs I know, you may have a stack of books on your nightstand that haven't created actual change in your relationship with your finances, because they're not tied into your purpose. Specifically, the bridge between your business finances and your big *why* hasn't been built yet. Ultimately, what we're attempting to accomplish is to get you to a point where feeling uncomfortable about money is a thing of the past. Where dis-ease and real suffering have been put behind you. Wouldn't it feel fantastic to set yourself free from your financial stress as an entrepreneur?

To do so, we'll look at each stage of the Eight-Fold Path through the lens of money in the next chapters. At every step, there are exercises designed to increase your comfort around handling your finances, and I encourage you to take the time with each before you move on in the book. Every stage has a purpose and when brought together, this process allows us to establish a new relationship with our finances, looking at the practical and the emotional together to ultimately find our Middle Way, which I like to call *Zen Money*. To give you a sense of our journey, here are the stages we'll explore together:

- The Right Understanding: Finding Clarity
- The Right Thought: Gaining Perspective
- The Right Speech: Creating Happiness in Your Business
- The Right Action: Paying Yourself
- The Right Livelihood: Building Your Money Rituals

- The Right Effort: Becoming Empowered
- The Right Mindfulness: Training Your Brain
- The Right Concentration: Building Your Strategy
- The Middle Way: Finding Your Balance

We'll look at old money stories and how they're affecting your ability to successfully navigate the world today. We'll explore what's happening in your business today and ways to streamline your money management to your advantage. Plus, we'll discuss how to know if you can pay yourself (and how much!), and the tools you need to develop a financial strategy that *feels* fantastic in all areas of your life.

Are you ready to get started?

## Chapter 2

# The Right Understanding

*"The Future belongs to those who believe in the beauty of their dreams."*

**~ Eleanor Roosevelt**

You're champing at the bit to dive into everything, aren't you? Once we make the decision to learn more about an area that makes us a little uncomfortable, it's easy for our ego to jump in and attempt to absorb all the information *right now!* And while it may feel exciting to catapult ourselves into "how-to" stuff, we can't begin with that, because we first need to establish why we've decided to learn this in the first place. And not just a cursory glance, but a deeper dive into understanding our full picture around our financial goals. Starting with our "*why*" is the most important part of our *Zen Money* journey.

I like to call this step "finding clarity." For my readers who've done emotional and spiritual work, or received coaching of one kind or another, it won't come as a surprise that we need to start by looking at where we currently stand, in order to catalyze change. Finding clarity at this level is about getting connected to the very reason you jumped into the entrepreneurial waters in the first place.

## What's Your BIG DREAM?

I want you to consider a few things. Why are you in business? What's your *big dream*? Is it tied to your business or something outside of it? Many of us love being an entrepreneur, are happy giving all of ourselves to our work, and our big mission is driven by growing our business. And others of us say, "I'm doing this entrepreneurial thing because I like the flexibility and the money I make. But for me it's just a stepping stone to my *big vision*." Maybe you want to be able to pay off your mortgage and send your kids to college. That's a beautiful *why*. It's as good a *why* as wanting to build schools in Uganda or working to bring clean water to rural villages in South America or some other global initiative. The truth is, we all have a bigger sense of *why* behind our immediate goals as an entrepreneur. If we're not tapped into that, then the work of earning the money itself starts to become meaningless. It's not fun and we don't feel good about it, and we start to drift from our purpose.

It's important to think about your primary *why* (or *whys* … you can have more than one), because, without being truly clear on these big questions, it's supremely difficult to feel good about your financial flow. I define *financial flow* as the financial management required for success as a business owner. The wonderful thing about tapping into our *why* is that it breaks us from the habitual "should" we often feel around our money management. Many of us get to a certain point in our business where things are beginning to roll. Maybe you've hit multiple six figures and are starting to become fluent in the language of business. Perhaps you feel you know exactly what to do with your financial work, but it all feels like an unexciting "must" on your task list. Maybe you're approaching seven figures, but you secretly feel like a fraud among your entrepreneurial friends because you don't really know your numbers. Everyone knows that the financial pillar is extremely important in business, but let's be honest: That work often isn't very exciting, so maybe you haven't fully embraced it yet. It happens for many smart, capable entrepreneurs, so don't beat yourself up if this feels familiar. The point is that if we can tie our financial work to *why* we're working so hard as an entrepreneur, it helps change that "should" into a feeling of *Zen* about money management … and in all areas, not just your business.

From what I've seen, when people give up on entrepreneurship – because let's be honest, it's exceptionally hard – it's because they can't see a clear connection between the work that they're doing, the money that's coming from it or being spent because of it, and their big ultimate goals. If we can put a plan in place that ties all of these aspects of your life together, you're much more likely to continue growing successfully … a plan that's absolutely clear, makes sense to you, and *feels* great.

So how do we do that? We get our money picture fully aligned.

## Zen Money Means 360-Degree Integrity

For me, the idea of *Zen Money* really means having financial integrity in *all* areas of your life: in your business, on the personal side, and with your local or global giving. If we're doing well in our business, but we're not paying attention to our personal finances, then we're not in integrity. If we say our community (however we define that) is a priority, but we never find time or money to support the organizations we care about, then we're out of alignment, as well.

This is completely tied into your big *why*. I have a client whose *big dream* is to completely change how her peers view success in her country. She sees young people demoralized by limited employment opportunities and a cultural sway toward lassitude. A true entrepreneur at heart, she's building a fast-growing creative business in the online space and is extremely clear on her immediate, mid-term (three- to five-year), and long-term goals. Because she's so committed to building her own success in order to lead by example and to develop a platform from which to spread her big message in her country, she's become quite good at mitigating her financial fears. In fact, we started working together because she recognized that she couldn't continue to grow and achieve her dreams if she didn't know her numbers within the business at any given moment. Once a year at tax time would no longer do, so she bit the bullet and agreed to step into her discomfort around money in order to move past it and continue moving toward her goals.

Give yourself some time to envision your future self and what you'd like to achieve with all your hard work. What part of this entrepreneurial journey lights you up and gets you out of bed every morning? Your *big dream* will become the *why* to shift all those financial *shoulds* into something you look forward to knowing, because your money will be a lens through which you can gauge your progress to success.

---

## EXERCISE
# Your Financial Feeling State

To get started on this path to the Right Understanding, I want to offer you an exercise to determine your financial feeling state as an entrepreneur. It's short and easy to do. Simply have a pen and piece of paper handy, take a few deep breaths, close your eyes, settle into your body, and consider the following questions. For every answer, pay attention to your physical reactions and your gut responses on an internal level. In this exercise, the first answer is always the right one, so don't overthink it. The goal is to gauge your physical response on a scale of 1 to 10 (1 being "not at all," 10 being "absolutely!") of how true each statement feels to you. Simply read each question and note down your answers:

1. I'm completely confident managing my money.
2. I often question my spending decisions.
3. I'll do anything else before looking at my finances.
4. I love taking care of my money.
5. I don't know how to pay myself or how much without hurting my business.

6. It's easy to understand what needs to happen in my business around finances, and I'm comfortable with the language of money.

7. I have the tools in place I need to help me manage my money and my personal life.

8. I want money to feel abundant and easy.

9. I have a clear vision for my money, and how to use it to make a difference.

The purpose of this exercise is to establish a baseline on how you're feeling internally around your money management. We start with this exercise, so you have a reference point as you shift your understanding and relationship with money. If some of your answers bring up negative feelings or aren't where you'd like to be, then you have something to work on in the following chapters. It's a great way to start finding clarity around your money in a way that isn't just about "doing the right things," having a bookkeeper in place, or creating systems. Finding *Zen Money* for yourself is as much about the mental shifts we can make to *feel* better about money, as it is getting clear on the financial "ticky-tacky" work.

## S-U-F-F-I-C-I-E-N-C-Y – What Does It Mean to You?

While we're in this place of reflection, it's a great time to think how we might redefine the term "sufficiency." I don't know about you, but when I hear it, I immediately think of lack. "This is like barely breaking even. It's just barely enough. It's sufficient." It's right up there with "enough" and "paycheck-to-paycheck" as terms that make us feel small and unsuccessful.

But what if we could turn it on its head? What if we thought about sufficiency as being exactly what we need to feel great? For one person, that might be $100 a week. For another, the ability to feel great about their life might equal $1,000 a week. Redefining "sufficiency" in all aspects of our lives can be a watershed moment, because it can make an enormous difference in how we feel about our money situation. And as we know, feeling positive is more than half the battle. The actual dollar amounts don't particularly matter, if we are positively connected with our finances instead of having that millstone hanging around our neck.

Society tells us we're supposed to constantly be hungry around money ("I don't have enough. I never have enough. I need more.") and to feel its lack all the time. It's not a great way to live, but most of us learn it very early in life. The great news for us, though, is that we can redefine this conversation for ourselves, and in doing so, we can change our language around money in a way that *feels* better.

Consider for just a moment what "enough" really means to you. Does it mean living with your current couch because you don't really need another one (even if it's not a perfect match to your living room)? Or delaying an upgrade to a new software platform for your business? If you opted to wait, where would you allocate the money you've been setting aside for these expenses? What else can you do with those funds? And most importantly, how would that feel? These kinds of questions can help you start to establish a new version of "sufficient" in your life that may surprise you.

I have a client who realized that, as she was making leaps in her business, her old self kept wanting to bring her back to a safe, comfortable place that felt familiar. Her reaction was directly tied to her new understanding of sufficiency and old spending patterns. She realized that she'd been feeling the need to hoard things like candles and books. She told me she felt like she was a squirrel in winter, stashing away her acorns. Her gut told her the purchases would make her feel better, because in the past such a splurge would have felt extremely abundant. Now, however, the seventeen unread books and five unlit candles on her shelf felt like a mistake, because her new, current self knew that her urge to spend was really a fear response to the new, exciting strides she was taking in her business. She had redefined "sufficiency" but it took a little while for her old habits to catch up.

My goal for you is to redefine "sufficiency" from a negative, loaded connotation to a goal that allows for growth in other areas of your life. Because if we can be efficiently sufficient in one area, we'll have resources to put toward our big *whys* in our business, our personal life, and in our communities at large.

## Bear Brain: An Introduction

Do you know that feeling you get when faced with a problem? When your mind is running a mile a minute and you start to feel panicky? I'm sure you know what I mean. It crops up every single time we take on a new project or start to envision a new horizon for ourselves, our business, our world, which as entrepreneurs means every other day sometimes! I like to call this fun experience "bear brain," and I've spent a lot of time living in that space. I won't lie, it's pretty painful, because it amounts to my mind causing a stress response in my body as if a bear were attacking me and about to eat my face.

The truth is that there *is* no bear and there *is* no face eating! But if you're about to launch a new program or give a speech or sign a big new client or write a book or do *anything* that you don't currently recognize as something you know how to do, *bear brain* raises its ugly head. And man, can it get ugly!

In Zen Buddhism, this is called monkey brain. It's when your head, as you're taking in new information, or trying a new activity, decides that the whole concept is scary, and we spin out. Our mind goes into chatter mode, telling us "You need to run. Or fight. *Do something* to alleviate this discomfort!" That response is embedded in our DNA as a way of keeping us safe (i.e., don't do anything new because it's scary), and we often react to it in actual uncomfortable physical ways.

I'm sure you've encountered your own version of *bear brain* as an entrepreneur and I bring it up because we'll use this concept throughout the book. It's a way to check yourself against self-sabotage as you become the person who manages your finances effortlessly and joyfully. *Bear brain* often crops up around money, and we don't even realize it half the time. We try to keep ourselves safe, in a zone of understanding that's comfortable. Unfortunately, it doesn't really serve as us entrepreneurs when we're having to make decisions and constantly try new things to continue building on our success.

You'll see bear brain crop up in a multitude of ways: Can I afford to pay the rent? What if I lose my job? I really want to take that vacation, but I don't feel like I can make it happen financially, and I'm stressed out about it.

One thing I want you to realize about the old *bear brain* is that we have a choice about how we handle it when it shows up. You can succumb to the fear or you can decide to acknowledge it and move on. ("Oh hey, *bear brain* … you're doing that thing you do so well, but I'm going to ignore you, because I know that I just have to take a deep breath and move forward anyway.") This second response is the most effective way to handle *bear brain*, but it can take a while to make it a comfortable habit.

You can also think of *bear brain* in terms of the main tenet of Right Understanding. At its core, this step of the Eight-Fold Path is about creating kind thoughts versus ill will. To move away from negativity toward a positive flow of energy. For me, *bear brain* is ill will trying to take over by crying "What, what, what? I can't see where we're going, so it must be *bad*!" Negativity reigns supreme. But, we don't need to stay in that uncomfortable, fearful place. We can take a deep breath, and ask ourselves "Am I actually going to die over this decision?" Most often, the answer is "probably not" and if we recognize these situations when they crop up, we can quiet that frenetic, fearful voice. How? By putting a strategy around it.

*Bear brain* will certainly come up as you begin to examine your relationships and rituals with money. I guarantee it. And it'll probably pop up when you least expect it. The best way I know to handle it is to give yourselves a little bit of space to breathe and be kind to yourself, while continuing to get your financial house in order, whatever your mind may be telling you in an attempt to scare you off.

## REFLECTION QUESTIONS

1. What did you learn from doing the Financial Feeling State assessment?

2. Where does *bear brain* show up most often for you? How do you normally handle it?

3. How might you apply the concepts of The Right Understanding to your life right now?

---

## EXERCISE
# Your Money Goals

Part of finding your Zen includes getting comfortable with your actual numbers, and to begin talking about the nitty-gritty of your money picture, we need to set some goals. Why? Because it's hard to set a plan in place and develop a fantastic strategy if we don't know where you ultimately want to go. You need a road map, if true change is to happen for you, so this exercise is an important one on our path to *Zen Money*.

The point is to establish goals for yourself on a personal level, a relationship level, a business level, and on a community level. These four aspects can encompass your whole money vision. Taken together, if the money is flowing well and your needs are being met in each area financially, you'll feel truly fantastic about your money outlook. So, in this exercise, look at each category and establish at least two goals (and no more than four).

You may reflect on your personal money situation and realize that you're tired of not saving for retirement. It really makes you feel uncomfortable, so you decide to make a change in this area. You might want to commit to better self-care with monthly massages and make a plan to support that financially. It can be anything that sings to you. The whole fun of this exercise lies in looking at what isn't currently feeling good around money, and how you want to change it. How can we turn it 180 degrees, so it becomes something you *want* to do instead of something you want to ignore?

Think of this in terms of "I want x in place of y." For example, you might write "I want to start saving for retirement instead of ignoring it and feeling like I'm missing the boat on something." We could leave it there, but it's even more meaningful to drill down another level and determine why this new commitment is important to you. In this example, you might feel saving for retirement is important because you would like to have zero money worries later in life. Then we need to decide when you want to attain this outcome, because if we put an actual dated goal down, it's more likely to happen. Perhaps you're to stop avoiding your retirement and fully fund your Roth IRA by the end of this year, for example.

After you determine your personal, relationship, business, and community goals, let's add a value to each. Is there a dollar amount we can associate each goal, or an intrinsic value? You know how in meditation you picture something that isn't going well, and then you release it, and replace it with something else? In this exercise, we replace what's not feeling good with our new money vision: the things and situations that we want.

You're likely to come up with very practical items, like paying off the credit card debt you accumulated when starting your business. But if your secret desire is to buy a Lamborghini for yourself, then put that down as well. This exercise is all about dreaming and letting ourselves open to possibility around money, so don't hold yourself back here, not on the personal level or the relationship level. (Chances are good you have some kind of money reality that doesn't feel great in one or more of your relationships. This is a great time to ponder that and consider that.)

At the business level, this exercise might include a goal of building a cash buffer so you have six months of expenses covered at all times. As an entrepreneur, looking at your business financial goals feel a little more clear-cut and simple, but please go through all parts of this exercise anyway. After you've established your business goal(s) around money, add another one or two for community, because so many of us want to make a difference in our world. This might be at the local level, or perhaps there's an online global charity that you're interested in supporting or an organization doing good work in a different country that you've always wanted to support. Perhaps your community goal is to help 1,000 succeed in whatever your sphere of influence happens to be. The variations are endless; I encourage you to dream big.

This exercise will help you establish concrete financial goals that are linked to all areas of your life in meaningful ways. When we establish specific goals in each area, it's easier to make financial change happen and ultimately to feel great about our achievements.

## EXERCISE
# Indefinable You

This second exercise is a bit more organic. Sit down, get comfortable, and give your mind time to get quiet. Ponder your qualities as an entrepreneur that benefit you. We all have what I like to call "indefinable assets" – aspects that are of intrinsic value in our lives. We tend to discount them and now is the perfect time, before we dive into the hard numbers, to connect with our "other" assets. For example, I'm good at getting a lot of things done in a very short amount of time. It took me decades to recognize that intrinsic asset within myself, and still longer to feel comfortable saying it out loud. You might be great at connecting people, teaching others a difficult subject, or connecting the dots strategically. Most of us are taught to be careful of tooting our own horns and it's hard to speak about our strengths, but these non-numerical assets are of great value!

So, take a minute to think about what positive qualities you have as an entrepreneur that aren't specifically monetary. Then consider the flip side: What qualities do you have that might be detrimental to your success? We'll call these liabilities (although I do think that many times a little learning can minimize these negative traits a great deal). We can change and expand on our intrinsic assets and liabilities, depending on our focus and approach. What do you have working in your favor (assets), and what traits might be holding you back (liabilities)?

Just take five or ten minutes, and free write about it. Then review it and note if any part is money- or value-related. We do this exercise so that you can start to see where energy might be leaking, and to identify what's supporting your efforts that you can build upon. Just this one exercise can significantly change your definition of value.

## Bottom Line

Throughout this book, we'll be using a very simple approach to help establish your money habits, peel back the layers of your financial discomfort, and build up your money confidence. And it all starts with understanding what's happening now and comparing it to where we want to be in the future. Fully defining our goals and looking at what makes us tick is an important first step. Getting crystal clear on what we want for ourselves financially, looking at what might attempt to hold us back, and acknowledging it consciously will allow us to implement the ideas in the following chapters in a meaningful way.

Chapter 3

# The Right Thought

*"Each of us has an inner thermostat setting that determines how much love, success, and creativity we allow ourselves to enjoy. When we exceed our inner thermostat setting, we will often do something to sabotage ourselves, causing us to drop back into the old, familiar zone where we feel secure."*

**~ Gay Hendricks**

A boiled-down version of the Right Thought in Zen Buddhism might be described as "developing a resolve to commit to this path." For our conversation, I see it as agreeing to a shift in our relationship with money and gaining a little perspective. Just as you would make a conscious commitment to exercise or to eat healthier, this stage of our *Zen Money* path is about diving into what we *think* our relationships are with money (because we all have several) and seeing that the stories we've carried about our spending and earning habits might be far different from our reality.

Why? Because when we're able to look at where we've been and see clearly where we stand now, we can decide where we want to go. You set some broad level goals in the last chapter, and now we're going to delve into *how* we interpret money in our lives and where we can tweak things to set ourselves up for success. To do so, we have to do just a *little* bit of backward looking before we can lock in a solid, forward-looking plan.

Interestingly enough, this is true with finances, too. Most of the time the financial world is backward looking. It's based on data that we must generate before we can analyze and make decisions from it. That can be frustrating, especially for entrepreneurs who like to think, *I know where I want to go, let's just get started already*! All this rearview pondering can seem like a waste of time. Here's the thing, though … we have to look behind us first to suss out what's actually been going on. It might be quite different than what we thought. Once we establish a really clear vision from our actual numbers, we can build a solid strategy to move us forward.

## Managing Money with Grace

The key to doing this effortlessly is to review without judgment. Stripping away the urge to layer an emotional response over our finances allows us to understand ourselves as we truly are. It's important because with money matters in particular, we often carry shame, worry, doubt, and mistrust in ourselves. We place value judgments on the decisions we're making and even on the numbers themselves, when the reality is our numbers are just a tool. They're static. So, if we can separate ourselves from those feelings of guilt and take in the information with an open mind, we're less emotionally attached and can make much better decisions because we're actively looking at and utilizing our numbers.

Hence the need for a little perspective. If we can agree simply to not beat ourselves up too much about what we discover over the next few chapters as we look at your money situations, this will be better and more productive for you. As entrepreneurs, we have big, big dreams. Part of building your empire includes getting hyper clear on your specific money goals. I encourage you to be wildly curious with zero judgment of what you find (and go ahead and ditch the self-flagellation while you're at it).

## Let's Flip Your Money Story

So, how do we turn our negative money story on its head? In my boat, it all starts with looking at our old money relationships. You know the *bear brain* I talked about in the last chapter? We'll continue looking at how it might show up as we move along our path to *Zen Money*. The reality is, for a lot of us, these old money stories stick like a broken record until and unless we release them. *Even if they're patently not true*! It can show up in thoughts that sound something like this:

"Nope. Change around money isn't possible; this is just my reality. I was led to believe at an early age that I was never going to earn enough money to support myself." Lo and behold, you find yourself as an adult unable to support yourself because that story was planted in your head.

I had a client who told me that as a young girl (maybe ten or eleven), she asked her father (a successful banker) to teach her about money, because she was interested in learning how it worked. He told her, "Oh honey, your job is to marry somebody who's going to take care of you, so you don't need to know about money." That one belief – implanted early and deeply – stuck with her for decades. She lived for years with a horrible relationship around money and a pile of limiting beliefs about what she could and couldn't do in her life because of that one conversation. It stayed with her and affected her ability to grow, to earn at her at fullest potential, and to generally just feel good around money. The hardest part about that story was that, years later, she brought up this exchange with her father, and he had *zero* recollection of it and couldn't believe he'd ever said such a thing. Two completely different perspectives on a short interaction led to years and years of money shame, guilt, and confusion.

Many of us have something like this in our proverbial financial closet. You may not even realize that those stories are there, hanging out in your subconscious. And I can guarantee that they're absolutely affecting how you interact with money today.

## Gift of Receiving

Let's take just a minute here and talk about the gift of receiving. Generating income is the driver of your business, but there are ways to trip ourselves up when it comes to collecting our cash. I'm sure you're familiar with the gift of giving and its benefits, but the art of receiving is equally important. It can be difficult to master as an entrepreneur. We're often raised with a certain discomfort in being on the receiving end of things. I don't know about you, but I was raised to believe that you take care of yourself, stand on your own two feet, and pull yourself up by your bootstraps. While it's a great way to learn to be self-sufficient, it can make it hard to learn to receive gracefully. And ultimately it can impact our ability to grow our businesses to its fullest potential.

Here's a little story that might be a useful illustration of this phenomenon. I learned from my mother that giving was the best thing you could do as a human being. If there was an opportunity to bring an unexpected gift to a friend, you should do it. Picking up the check was the norm, and as a young adult, I often went out of my way to treat friends, saying "I'll just grab this, no big deal." Holy moly, did that get me into trouble financially! I couldn't seem to stop because I only knew how to give – I was actively uncomfortable when the tables were turned. I wanted to show those I loved how much I valued them by literally spending my resources away, because I'd been taught that giving was more important than receiving.

Fast forward to my life as an entrepreneur. The drive to never ask for help, to give but not receive, made it extremely difficult to feel confident establishing fair pricing strategies and set appropriate payment expectations. Intellectually, I knew how important setting these parameters is for any business, but if anyone asked for an exception, it was extraordinarily hard for me to stick to my guns. Many of my clients have this same impulse, and likely this rings true for you as well.

Have you ever tried to breathe out without breathing in? Try it … it's impossible. You get blue in the face, and you simply need to breathe in at some point. If you go too long doing only one or the other, you can't function well. Money works in the same way. If you're only spending and not receiving in your business or your personal life, your cash flow becomes choppy and uncertain. If you're always receiving and never spending, your focus becomes as narrow as Scrooge and you lose your zest for your work and life in general, as your interest in your income becomes fear-driven.

However, if we can breathe in and out in constant flow, we can not only survive, we can thrive. Learning the art of receiving is a big part of creating this in your life. Consider how good you are at receiving right now. Does it come naturally or is it uncomfortable? Do you find yourself making unsound financial decisions around your income strategies that might be based in a deeper-seated discomfort with receiving? Do you expect the universe to provide and then it does? Many of us are not that attuned to the concepts of manifestation and the energy-exchange side of the money, and receiving it feels tricky. For some of us, this discomfort may be tied up in money that feels toxic. If you have cash coming in but it's from a source that has bad memories associated with it or we have a poor relationship with the person giving, it can feel unhealthy. However, when we're aligned with our income, the ability to receive becomes as natural and positive as breathing.

I want you to think about how that looks in your life now. If receiving money doesn't feel like a nice gentle inhale, consider why that might be. Are there areas where we can establish parameters, so the receiving part of your business feels better? That likely includes the emotional piece of the receiving puzzle as well as your contract-to-cash process, which we'll discuss in the next chapter. Ultimately, we want a clear and streamlined process for our invoicing and collections, plus plans for any money coming in. Are we giving our cash a specific job to do?

And even before that, ask yourself "What's it like to receive it?" Does it feel fantastic or does it immediately seem like it's not enough? This happens to an incredible number of people. You sign a client and you're ecstatic for maybe five seconds and then your mind moves on, fretting about what's coming next. All because we're not great at receiving, trusting in the actual process of money coming in and *feeling* positive about it.

What would make it easier for you to breathe money in as easily as you take in air? Find a quiet place and consider this. Think about where money has come from in the last six months. Did you have to chase clients down to get it in the door? Did it arrive in a way that felt a little uncertain or perhaps by the time it showed up, you were already on to other things and didn't take time to stop and appreciate it? Are you "forgetting" to follow up with clients and leaving money on the table? When that happens, we're energetically declaring that being paid isn't a priority. And then we may immediately find a way to spend it, particularly if we don't have a plan for it. Some of us instinctively try to push our negative associations away by literally ridding ourselves of the cash, without benefit to our business or our personal lives.

My goal in asking you these questions is to help you recognize your feelings around receiving and establish new reactions that feel natural and unburdened by questions of self-worth. None of us need to prove our value by receiving money, but we often unconsciously try to do just that when left to our old money stories. And letting money "happen" to you, including sales and income, means a chaotic and unstable relationship with your finances.

I have a client who has a great niche and fabulous personality, and enough financial education and savvy to have sky-rocketed her business. Right out of the gate, everyone thought she had everything necessary (expertise, charisma, drive) to build huge revenue in short order. But it didn't happen. Despite knowing her numbers intimately and having plans in place at every turn for how she would use her income to grow her business and support her life, a poor "breathe in" habit stopped her from attracting and keeping the clients she was targeting.

What was going on? It turns out that, deep down, she was insecure about the value she was providing her clients (which by all accounts was enormous), so she was showing her receiving discomfort in the form of blowing sales calls, lowering her prices more than she intended, and allowing potential clients to set payment terms that were to their advantage but not hers (no win-win scenarios). Her ship-shape and frugal expenses were irrelevant to her business growth because her ability to receive income was hampered. It was a case where having a great money management plan was completely undermined by discomfort with receiving part of her financial flow. And as we all know, if there's no money coming in, we have an expensive hobby, not a business.

Luckily, once we both realized what was happening, she was able to make a conscious change in her relationship around bringing in money and everything started growing in her business just as everyone had predicted. Within three months, she'd hit her original income goals and was on track for multiple six-figure growth for the year. Not because she tapped into a new client pool or because she took out extra Facebook ads. All because her energy around her ability to "breathe in" shifted. It can happen for you, too, if you give your receiving process a little love and attention.

## What Kind of CEO Are You?

In addition to recognizing our habits around generating income, it's important to identify how we handle money as an entrepreneur. During my career working with small business owners, I've come to realize there are two types of entrepreneurs: those who use their numbers voraciously and those who "shoot from the hip," making decisions based on their intuition. There are pros and cons to each approach. Obviously, as a numbers woman myself, I tend to believe that the more information you have at your fingertips, the better off you'll be in the decision-making process. That being said, I've known plenty of successful entrepreneurs whose gut was spot on 98% of the time, as well.

Ideally, I'd love for you to have a balance of both, so your financial decision-making becomes a mix of data-driven and that hard-to-define "knowing" that many of the entrepreneurs I know have in spades. Since we're looking for a middle path in our journey to *Zen Money*, this hybrid is the holy grail, in my opinion.

A lot of people deal with their money in a very intuitive way. They have a gut sense of what will work, how to set pricing strategies, and what is a manageable expense. I'm the same way, strange to say, but I always go back and double check the numbers to make sure I didn't miss something in the moment. If you're wired to leap before you look, double-checking your sixth sense against what your finances are actually telling you is a great idea. Alternately, if you find yourself being unable to make a decision without reams of data to support it, you might benefit from putting your gut to work a bit more.

So, I'd like you to take a moment and reflect on how you've made financial decisions up to this point. Have you tended to throw down the credit card and hope for the best? Or do you know to the penny whether you can afford a new training program or attend that event with the movers and shakers? How does your decision-making *feel*? If it's uncertain and fear-based, then we have some work to do, and getting a little more intimate with the inner workings of your business finances is the path to changing that around. But don't worry! We won't throw your creative, intuitive, organic self out the window either. If relying on your instincts has brought you a level of success, then it would be foolish to attempt to strip that away entirely. Think of this as an add-on to your inherent assets exercise from the last chapter. What are your traits around monetary decisions as an entrepreneur and how can we build on them to your financial advantage?

When you've considered where you are today as a CEO, and where you might ultimately like to be, give yourself a pat on the back. You've just done some serious reflection work that many business owners never accomplish. Hopefully, it will begin to open the door to understanding your business money picture with greater clarity.

## Bear Brain: Old Stories Are True

How does *bear brain* show up as we're establishing the Right Thought around our money? Generally, as the belief that our old money stories are unchangeable. That the story that we can't possible earn more than our parents, or that we're bad at managing our money is 100 percent true and can never be otherwise.

It can be very uncomfortable to confront our old, embedded stories about money, particularly if they're negative ones. We self-sabotage to keep them true and find ourselves questioning why we can't get past a certain point in our earning or wondering why it's so hard to make ends meet. If this sounds familiar, I encourage you see it as *bear brain* and move on in your financial education anyway. Remember: *Bear brain* is there to keep us safe, but it can't recognize when our old tales about our ability to manage money are outdated and untrue. Looking closely at those stories in the following exercises will help clear the *bear brain* once and for all.

## REFLECTION QUESTIONS

1. Are you committed to making a change in your life around money?

2. What comes up as you begin to delve into your financial perceptions?

3. Have you ever considered how your view of money might be holding you back from success?

--- **EXERCISE** ---
## Your Money Story

Since some of the stories that you're carrying around with you are likely no longer serving you, I want you to just take a few minutes to sit quietly and just let yourself breathe into a quiet place and think back to your earliest money memory. We all have them. It might be that your grandfather gave you a five-dollar bill for your fifth birthday and that was the first time you had money for yourself. It might be remembering your mother worrying about how to pay for groceries or watching your father struggle with taxes. All kinds of images can come up, including great money memories. Look and listen to the details of that event, and let it just soak in. Then, let it come up to your consciousness, and write down what you saw and how it made you feel.

After you do that first round, I want you to check back and really see if there's anything else that comes up when you just let your mind flow, think about money, and your relationship with it. Something that you learned as a teenager with your first job, perhaps. Write down what comes up. The goal is to look at what may be weighing you down around money, and how you can redefine it for yourself. As you look at the stories popping up for you, look if there are any correlations between those old stories and how they made you feel, and how you make financial decision now as an entrepreneur and in your personal life. Do you find anything surprising? Are there any parallels there?

Consider whether any of those stories are true, or if they were implanted accidentally and have no real basis in reality. Simply recognizing them often will help their power simply dissipate into the breeze, leaving you clean and ready to replace them with new, purposeful thoughts that will help you go further instead of holding you back.

## —— EXERCISE ——
# Current Money Picture

Remember how I said we weren't ready to dive into the "ticky-tacky" yet? Here's the caveat: I'd like you to follow the Old Money Story exercise with a look into your current money picture. This is where you can start delving into your actual financial data. To develop a clear strategy, we have to start pulling some numbers for you to work with, from both your business and your personal life. I want you to think about how you're currently managing your finances, and how it feels. And, what would you like to change, if anything?

This exercise is designed to help you get clear on what's working and where you might be able to put some improvements in place so that you're feeling a lot more empowered around your money. I also want you to start collecting some actual data you'll want to have on hand as you work through the next few chapters. For this, we'll need at least three months' worth of income and expenses for your business (six months would be better, so you can start to see trends). Also, list out the balances you have in your checking and saving accounts for the business or in your personal life, and anything you might have in terms of assets – things of value – and liabilities – anything we owe other people, like a credit card balance or loan. Note them separately, if possible.

Sidebar: If your business and personal accounts aren't yet split out, do the best you can here, but make plans to create accounts so you can start seeing your business apart from your personal finances. This is a step on your path to *Zen Money*. If you've already taken it, congratulations!

For example, your details might include a personal checking account with $2,500 in it and a savings accounts with a $500 balance. You may have two credit cards with balances of $1,800 and $10,600 respectively. You may have a system in place that gives you that information easily, from a Profit & Loss Statement (showing your income, expenses, and net profit) and a Balance Sheet (showing your assets, liabilities, and equity). We'll use all that information in the following chapters, and if you have an easy way to grab it already set up, fantastic. Don't panic if you don't, though. You just need to be able to grab your financial information. If you're reading this book, you're likely already running a business, which means you have some kind of bookkeeping or financial tracking in place, so there should be a way to grab these numbers.

It's important to look at this information to make changes that will raise your entrepreneurial game. Going through these exercises will allow you to see what's been happening, with the money in your business and personal life, right now, and that first review will help springboard you into the next work of the upcoming chapters.

## Bottom Line

We can't begin to shift our financial reality without a clear understanding of where we've been (and how it's affecting us now) and where we are today. Looking at the misconceptions and old stories we're carrying around money is the best way to start peeling back the layers of our financial relationships. That can include early childhood lessons as well as stories we tell ourselves today as entrepreneurs.

The best way to change those stories is to look at their roots and gauge our current reality against them. I encourage you to take as much time as you need to dig into your money stories. Write down what you find. Consider how those lessons may be playing out in your life right now. When your money patterns become clearer, the task of drawing your current money picture will be a piece of cake. And once you have a handle on what's happening around money in your life, you'll be better able to use your numbers to your advantage.

## Chapter 4

# The Right Speech

*"What you pay attention to grows. If you are attracted to negative situations and emotions, then they will grow in your awareness."*

**~ Deepak Chopra**

D o you cringe when you're in a room with other entrepreneurs and someone starts talking about ROI and throwing around terms like positive cash flow, debt consolidation, and tax deferment? A lot of people I know are in a limbo state when it comes to their business finances this way. They want to appear savvy with all this business-y type stuff, but they're not quite sure how to start getting comfortable with the lingo, much less use it to their advantage.

How do you go from secretly hoping someone doesn't ask you for your numbers in your next mastermind meeting to feeling confident and at ease? You learn how to step fully into the role of CEO of your company. It's the first stage of finding your full *Zen Money* and I call it "creating happiness in your business."

In *Zen*, the idea of the Right Speech includes thoughtful communication to unite and avoid dissention (even with yourself). Being resolved to speak kindly and without anger can move us closer to everyday, compassionate living. So often, we have a little voice in our head whispering that we're not doing it right, that if we make a mistake around our money we're a failure, and all kinds of other negative self-talk. It *is* possible, though, to shut that voice down, and create a beautiful relationship with money in your life. And as an entrepreneur, it all starts with your business.

This concept of developing how we talk about money and being mindful around our finances is way to move us away from the *should* and into the *want*. Most of you likely are doing many things "properly" from a financial standpoint already, and I am going to assume that you have a few systems in place that keep your contract-to-cash cycle humming along, and your cash flow on track, but even if you don't have that sorted out yet, these concepts still apply.

Many entrepreneurs I know are stumped when it comes to looking at their numbers, if and when they receive their reports, even with a bookkeeper to help them out, or a knowledgeable VA tracking income and expenses. If that feels familiar, don't worry! We're going to dive into what exactly you need to make smart, strategic decisions for your business, and speak the language of business finance a little more fluently.

But first, let's talk about where you're at on your Entrepreneurial Journey.

## Your Business Lifeline

Just as in life, there are stages to business we all go through – a reliable growth process that, once you're aware of it, can help you to stop feeling at loose ends around your money decisions. When we first start on our Entrepreneurial Adventure, we create what I like to call our Business Baby. In this stage, our newborn business requires a great deal of time and effort, and from a financial standpoint, you are feeding it from your own pocket. We dip into savings, or use the proceeds of a sale of assets, take out a loan, or use credit cards to get started. This phase is uncomfortable for most of us. We're excited but we're also nervous watching the money flow out of the door in seemingly unstoppable waves. It's easy to get caught up in an overspending mindset in this stage, because we're learning the ropes and everyone else around us appears to be using expensive platforms and things, so we think we need those tools, too. (Hint: This is *bear brain* at work.) Many people get hung up around their money initially in this stage by overextending their financial reach without much of a real strategy before they're making a single penny.

The next phase is the Business Teenager. Your business is making some money and you're able to pay for the expenses you're incurring for your work, so you're no longer losing money, but there's not much of a pot left over to pay yourself, much less think about taxes. Your business can go to the fridge and feed itself, but it's self-absorbed and not capable of feeding you yet. This is a stage that many of us attempt to gloss right over without stopping and savoring the fact that we've grown a strapping, sustainable business capable of taking care of itself.

If you're in this phase and it's feeling uncomfortable, take a minute and revel in the fact that you've successfully created something viable and it's reached a point where it can stand on its own two feet!

The final stage, and our ultimate goal, is when our business becomes an adult. The Business Adult is bringing in income with additional opportunities for growth around every corner. Your business expenses are easily covered and you're able to not only set aside money for taxes, you're bringing home a healthy chunk of cash on a regular basis, too. When you finally reach this stage, it feels like nirvana, because the first two phases are so uncomfortable to go through. At this point, your business is feeding you, is capable of giving back to its community, and hopefully is an upstanding member of society. It's every parent's dream.

There's no rule as to how long it takes to move through these phases. I've seen entrepreneurs blow right through the first two stages in six months or less. I also know many people who get stuck in the Business Baby phase and never get out of it. They wind up giving up in frustration because the money simply isn't catching up and there's so much debt from the initial expenses that they simply fold it in and find something else to do. I think this is tragic – when so much creative potential goes to waste because of a poor understanding of and relationship with money.

I don't mean to sound judgey here. I've been through these phases myself and I know how easy it is to fall prey to our fears and believe that just one more program or tool will be the magic trick to making everything fall into place. The issue is that, if we're trying to live on our proceeds before we even have them (jumping directly into the Business Adult phase), then we've missed a critical step in our business growth and we might have to backtrack to establish a solid financial foundation that will allow for the growth we really want. This pendulum swing can make you queasy. It's far more sustainable to establish your financial footing in the beginning (as much as possible) so once you hit the Business Adult phase, there's no going back.

How do you know what a solid financial foundation looks like for *you*? All we need is a little basic math….

## A Simple Equation

Throughout the rest of this book, we'll keep coming back to a very basic formula as we peel back the layers in your financial house. And I'm going to keep repeating this financial equation over again until it stops seeming like a foreign language and starts feeling like an old, reliable friend.

The financial equation looks like this: *Income − Expenses = Profit*. I'm sure you've seen it before. When it comes to making decisions around our finances in our business, this is the place to start. If we don't have enough income to cover our expenses, there is no profit. And profit in our business is the bridge to our personal finances.

I want you to be intimately familiar with this basic math, even if you self-identify as a non-numbers person. It's how you'll battle *bear brain* when it crops up around your big decisions as a business owner. I happen to love getting information because it calms my mind and makes me feel more secure. I get that not everyone feels better having more data in front of them.

However, in this instance, coming back to what your numbers are telling you is paramount to your continued financial success.

This basic equation works for another part of our financial picture as well: the value within our company. Most people, when they start their business, are solely focused on their income and expenses, and driving profit to the bottom line. What takes a while to bring into the conversation is how that relates to our company's increase or decrease in overall health. We find this in our assets (anything we have of value) and our liabilities (anything we owe other people). The second version of the financial equation looks like this: *Assets – Liabilities = Equity*. Does it look familiar? It should. In finance, we're consistently taking our positives (income and assets), subtracting out the negatives (expenses and liabilities), and seeing what's left over to play with. In this instance, the equation simply means that the more we increase our holdings (think checking accounts, accounts receivable, fixed assets, or anything we could turn into cash if need be) and the more we limit our liabilities (think outstanding credit card balances or loans), then the greater the value we've created in our business (i.e. equity).

The two equations go together in a simple way. The more profit we have, the more equity we generate. And typically, the money we take out of the business for ourselves comes from the equity pool. That is, the more we have "left over," the more money can flow to our personal lives, which is why we went into business in the first place, right? Think of it this way: We can't take out value from the company if our liabilities are too high without further devaluing our business. Alternatively, we can easily pay ourselves and continue to grow the business if we can generate sufficient profits. We'll continue to work with this math, but for now consider what your financial equations are currently telling you. Are you in the negative in profit, but still taking money out for your personal life? If so, you're likely putting yourself back into the Business Teenager stage without realizing it. Are you increasing your value in the business but afraid to pay yourself anything? If so, you're likely not feeling that great about your business and all your hard work is feeling pretty stressful. Both are common extremes when we first start getting traction in our businesses, and we're looking to move to a middle ground through a closer look at what your numbers are telling you.

But first we need to identify what stage of your Entrepreneurial Adventure you're currently navigating.

## Take a Dive

So how do we recognize whether we're in the Business Baby, Teenager, or Adult stages, and work within them strategically while still putting food on the table? It all comes down to those reports I mentioned in the last chapter: your Profit & Loss Statement and your Balance Sheet. Now that you have the financial equation firmly rooted in your mind, it's time to look at what these reports are telling you. Just as we looked at your money stories that may be holding you back from success, your numbers themselves have a story to tell. It's our job to listen and adjust our financial habits and decisions, based on what they relay.

Imagine if you bought a house without getting an inspection first. You could wind up finding you need a new roof, the furnace is shot, and there's a mold problem in the basement. You wouldn't jeopardize your savings with a down payment, would you? Your business finances are no different, and yet many of us take a similar risk when we fail to really look at what's happening on a month-to-month basis.

When was the last time you looked at your Profit & Loss Statement? Remember, that can be as simple as tracking your income (money you've earned) and expenses (money you've spent) in a spreadsheet or a notebook. If you're not checking in on a regular basis, you're missing an opportunity to build the financial house of your dreams. So, go ahead and pull your P&L from the past month (or three) and look at what it's telling you. You probably already have a sense of where you stand, but double-check anyway. You might be surprised at what you find. Are you making more money than you realized, so you have extra to play around with inside the business (or more to take out for your own pocket)? Has the past quarter been harsher than you'd anticipated, and you need to up your marketing game? When you look at your reports regularly, your money story will become clearer and you'll be able to make financial decisions with more confidence because you're intimately familiar with your numbers. So, let's get cozy with them! (We'll talk more in Chapter Six about how to build great habits around analyzing your money.)

## Allocation of Abundance

Okay, so what happens once we're wide open to receiving and the money's flowing into our businesses? Money gurus often talk about allocating resources. Simply put, that means making choices about how we utilize our resources. And a lot of times, this kind of talk feels deeply imbedded in lack. There never seems to be enough to go around, does there? Or we might have reserves, but they're inaccessible, just as we have plenty of food to feed the world's population, but it's so unevenly distributed that we have obesity and starvation living side by side in the same communities. We'll continue to talk about the allocation of your resources throughout the book, but for now I want you to focus on what's happening in your business around your monetary abundance (or your perceived lack of it). When you looked at your numbers, what did you see? Did it appear as plenty and opportunity, or did you feel limitations?

The first step is recognizing where things stand right now. The second is creating and implementing a plan, which we can accomplish by working the financial equation to your advantage. You can do this in three ways:

1. *Maximize your contract-to-cash cycle.*
2. *Give your money a job to do.*
3. *Pay attention to your bottom line.*

Let's look at each of these a little further.

## Maximize Your Contract-to-Cash Cycle

Have you ever considered how your client on-boarding process may be holding you back? I talk about this in depth in *From Zero to Zen* but want to review it again here. If you're at all unclear or loose with establishing payment terms, not extremely clear about what services you provide (and which you won't), or otherwise leaving money on the table, then you're not maximizing your contract-to-cash cycle. As we know, "cash is king" and the faster you can turn your work into money in pocket, the easier time you'll have meeting your immediate financial obligations and having cash on hand to pay yourself.

Look at how you bring on clients and whether there are ways to streamline the process so that your income flow is consistent. Do you offer several payment options? Perhaps you can cull that down to just two: lump sum up front or three monthly payments (with an additional cost to cover the cost of carrying their balance for them). Do you have a written contract that includes charging interest on late payments? Getting really clear on your financial rules will do two things: 1) It will help your clients because they'll clearly understand your process and mentally add additional value to your work because of it, and 2) You will *feel* better about enforcing it. When we don't have rules, every time we need to chase someone for money, we wind up feeling irritated at best, and disconnected from the client we're wanting to serve at worst. So, consider where you might tighten up your on-boarding process around money to be clear, get paid quickly, and ensure a smooth and fast transition to the important work you're doing. It'll make receiving the money feel better and allow you to be excited about working with new clients, because your process is clear, easy to communicate and execute, with better results all around.

## Give Your Money a Job to Do

Have you ever noticed that there never seems to be enough money left over at the end of the month? That might be a shortage of profit to pay yourself or to set aside for taxes. It might mean you're actually losing money (negative profit). Why does this happen to smart people? I see it frequently and I believe it's because many of us let our finances just "happen."

In other words, they happen to us, instead of us taking charge. I've found that entrepreneurs who are very clear on how much is coming in and have a plan for its allocation are the most successful at generating abundance (read: profit). Those who aren't, tend to find themselves without much left over to play with – or even, further in debt.

How does this work? It's because we're not giving our money a job to do. As with anything, money needs some boundaries to be fully successful. It's like this: If you're a parent and your child complains of being hungry, you have a choice. You can ask "What are you hungry for?" at which point your child will tell you brownies or candy. Or you can ask "Would you like carrot sticks or celery with peanut butter?" The first response is way too open-ended. The second sets some parameters around expectations.

We can apply the same philosophy to our finances. Instead of expecting to earn a vague amount of money (say five figures a month) that will generally cover our expenses and give us something to live on, we can get more specific with better results. What if you were to instead have a goal of earning $10,000 this month and a plan to set aside 30 percent for taxes in your savings account, pay all of your expenses (totaling $2,000), leave $1,000 in the business to create a cushion, and take the remaining $4,000 out as an owner's draw? A magical thing happens. Because we're looking at the details and giving our money specific jobs to do, instead of worrying whether we'll make ends meet or have enough, we're likely to exceed our goals. And if, for some reason, we don't hit our income numbers, we are much more likely to make fiscally responsible shifts in our spending and take-home expectations.

## Pay Attention to Your Bottom Line

Giving your money a job to do is closely tied to paying attention to your net profit (Remember our financial equation? This is what's left over). Most of us feel we're intimately aware of our profit (or lack thereof). However, do you really have a close personal relationship with your bottom line? Just like a tender bean plant in your garden, if you're not tending it diligently, it won't produce the bumper crop you're hoping for.

Without giving our money jobs to do, I can guarantee we're likely to not set aside anything for taxes, wind up spending all the cash on expenses that may not move our business forward and have nothing left over for ourselves. I had a client who had a brilliant business model and was considered an expert in her field. On the surface, it would appear that she was doing very well for herself. However, despite loads of income potential and client interest, she hadn't managed to do more than break even in the three years she'd been running her business. She even knew her numbers and understood how to swing the needle. What was the problem? Anything extra was always being eaten up, almost before she earned it, simply because she didn't have a plan for it. Every time she increased her income, her expenses miraculously went up, too, leaving nothing left over to grow her equity or be able to pay herself.

Or perhaps we're in the habit of pulling more cash out – and eating into our bottom line – than the business can sustain. I know entrepreneurs who, because of their perceived personal needs, take every penny of cash out of the business as soon as it comes in, without keeping any back to pay business expenses.

They wind up putting their business back in the Teenager or even the Business Baby stage, playing a shell game of moving money around, paying only the minimum on their credit cards, and having a hard time making ends on meet on all sides. This approach to your money hurts your ability to grow your value in the business itself. Remember that your bottom line is directly tied to the equity you're building. So, if we take it all out (or more) as an owner's draw (forgetting to set aside for taxes or expenses in the process), we're digging ourselves into an early fiscal grave. This happens to a lot of entrepreneurs, simply by not being intimate with their numbers.

Our business or our personal life can eat up our extra cash if we're not diligent, just as our kids will empty the cookie jar if left to their own devices. That could include purchasing things we don't need within the business, or taking out more money than we actually have, mostly based on not having a plan in place. A good way to manage this is to remember *why* we're working this hard in the first place. Likely it's not only to make a big impact in the world, it's also to support ourselves through our efforts. So, give your money jobs to do that keep your business viable (i.e. make sure you're covering your expenses, don't overspend on wants vs. needs, and have a plan for your debt) *and* allocate money for taxes and your personal pocket. (When I talk about paying yourself, I'm talking about a straight owner's draw to keep things simple. In this instance, the money you take out is not a business expense, but rather a reduction in your equity.) Keeping a steady focus on your bottom line will allow you to work within your plan, adjust as necessary, and build a strong, viable business.

When looking at your bottom line, keep two things in mind:

1.  You need to take taxes into consideration. A good rule of thumb is to set aside 30-40 percent of your cash receipts every month so you have money on hand to cover your quarterly and annual tax bills. (Check with your accountant to establish the appropriate percentage for your business.)

2.  If you follow Step #1 religiously, anything left over in your profit bucket becomes fair game for your pocketbook or to be reinvested in the business.

So, when we're trying to figure out how much we can pay ourselves – which is everyone's goal in the end, right? – paying attention to the bottom line is just as important as watching the top line (i.e. your income).

If you can think of your finances as separate buckets – business in one, and personal in another – then it's easy to visualize. Let's say your business income (cash that comes in) fills up your business bucket every month. You might have a little more one month, and a little less another, but whatever's in the bucket is what you have to work with. For complete peace of mind around your taxes (which I cannot recommend enough, because it's an area of huge stress for many entrepreneurs I know), pour out 30 percent of the water from your business bucket. If it was completely full, you've got 70 percent of the bucket left. If it was only three-quarters full this month, you'd pour off 30 percent of that. You can transfer that amount of money to a savings account and hold onto it until you need to pay a quarterly estimate or make up the difference at tax time.

Now we want to account for our business expenses. Let's say those are 25 percent of our total income, so you pour off another slug from the bucket. It's money that's out of our hands or already allocated. What's left over is what you have to play with, either in your personal life or to keep in the business as cash for future opportunities or to build your equity (value in the company).

Keep this image in mind; we'll come back to it in the next chapter when looking at how to manage the money you take out for your personal life. And now that you know the basic formula, what might get in the way to mess up your best-laid financial plans?

## Charging Your Worth

We've talked about what kind of tracking you should be prepared to do as a successful entrepreneur so now it's time to dig into one of the biggest topics that comes up in my work with my clients: setting your fees. Do you ever find yourself floundering when it comes to establishing your pricing? We all find it tough at times and go through times where we undercut our efforts by undercharging for our services. Why? Sometimes it's a fear of failure ("Let's make it easy for them to say yes,") and sometimes it's based on what outside sources are telling us about our value.

In either case, I've found that charging less is rarely the answer to financial stability when we have a service-based business. If you're uncomfortable naming your fee or find yourself consistently offering a lower rate than you'd like, I'm guessing it has to do with your discomfort around your numbers more than anything. Do you provide exceptional service? Do you care about your clients? If you're closing more new clients than not, there's likely room to increase your prices. I'd also argue that if your clients aren't getting the results you'd like to see, if they're not bought into the work you're doing together, then you're likely not charging enough.

Why not? In a twist of irony, the basic fact is that our clients will get more out of working with us if we charge a premium for our services. Think of all the low-ticket how-to tutorials you "invested" in as you started out in business. How much have you retained from the $49 video series on how to build your email list? What about that rock-bottom-priced assistant who ended up taking more of your time than it was worth and left you feeling that you'd be better off if you'd done it yourself (or maybe you *did* do all the work yourself)? At the end of the day, if you're not valuing yourself in your pricing, chances are your outcomes for your clients aren't great and you're not hitting your financial goals either. Your *bear brain* may be telling you that no one will pay what you want to charge, but that's frankly a complete lie. If you can solve someone's problem, whether you're a designer, a sales coach, or a wellness practitioner, and they trust that you're the person to do it, people will pay just about anything to make it happen. In other words, you may be telling yourself a story about your value as an entrepreneur. But don't worry … you can change this all around with a few simple tweaks.

And if you're finding it hard to make ends meet, your pricing is first place to start when looking to right your business's financial ship. You can come to your pricing numbers a couple of different ways: from the top down and the bottom up. Here's how it works...

## Top-Down Pricing

As business owners, our goal is to find our pricing sweet spot. In this method of building our fees, we need to do a little research into what other entrepreneurs are charging in our marketing space. You'll want to factor in your level of experience and qualifications, as well as the services you provide (just because someone you admire charges great money for their work doesn't mean you'll be able to match that right out of the gate).

Then, once you have a range of pricing in mind, consider what you're comfortable asking. I recommend working up to a number if your target price is hard to fathom saying out loud to a prospective client. For fun, let's say your target price is $5,000 for a 12-week training or coaching program and you're currently successfully charging $2,000. Over the next few months, you can increase your pricing until you're signing clients at that new fee. It can help you to quiet that inner voice that's saying, "But no one will pay me that much for just doing *xyz*!"

When pricing from the top down, we need to determine how much revenue we'll bring in at the new fee (based on an average of new work), then subtract out our average expenses and tax set-aside. What's left over? Does it leave you with enough money for your personal life to meet your needs? Does it feel sufficient? If not, it's time to go back to the drawing board with your numbers.

## Bottom-Up Pricing

We can use the exact same equation in reverse for bottom-up pricing. Determine how much you'd like to be able to take home from your business every month. Then add that number to your average business expenses. Finally, add in your tax set-aside. The total you come up with is your monthly income target. Based on the number of new clients or work you expect to bring in regularly, you can determine what your baseline pricing needs to be to allow you to bring home your ideal pay.

Not making sense? Let's look at an example: Let's say I want to be able to take $5,000/month out of my business and I have $3,500 in monthly expenses (averaged over the year to include big ticket items like a training program or event with travel costs). That means I need to generate at least $8,500/month in income. Fairly easy to do these days, right? Except we haven't accounted for taxes. So, we assume our $8,500 is 70 percent of the total income we require (the other 30 percent being our tax set-aside). To get our total revenue need, we divide $8,500 by 0.70 and come up with $12,143 (we'll round up to $12,500 for ease of the example). Now … how do we use this $12,500 income number to generate our pricing? If you can only take on five new clients a month, then you need to charge $2,500 per client. If you can take on eight clients, then you can drop your fees to $1,563 per client. Or perhaps you know $2,500 is the right price for your services and you see that you can work with more clients and generate more income than you originally thought. The beauty of it all is that the numbers will give you the answers and then *you get to decide!*

Using both of these strategies together, you'll find your sweet spot. Just be prepared to have it change frequently as you grow. While we like to tell ourselves stories about what we can and cannot charge for our services, the reality is that often when we increase our prices, the interest in our work grows as well.

A good friend of mine always cautions, "If you raise your rates, they'll just keep saying yes!" It's a tongue-in-cheek reminder that if you do great work and get results for your clients, the only limit to your pricing is in your own mind.

## Bear Brain: I Need It NOW!

As I came to the healthy conclusion of my battle with chronic Lyme disease, I worked with a mentor to help me establish a sustainable balance in my life using biohacking techniques (using your body's inherent skills to kick your wellness into overdrive) with enormous results. She once asked me if I were a robot. Obviously, the answer was "no" so she then went on to ask why I was acting like one. Her point was this: We're all trained to respond to external stimuli and over time, we start to think of it as the norm. But that kind of existence is frenetic and often uncomfortable, while paying attention to your internal reality and staying present there is a far more grounding and stable approach to managing our environment. This is true for our personal well-being *and* our financial health.

When we're in robot-mode, we're simply responding to external commands and demands. We do this with our finances all the time. I see it come up most often around what in today's lingo we call FOMO: the Fear of Missing Out. As entrepreneurs, particularly if you're in the online environment, FOMO is a real and insidious drag on our finances. And the kicker is this: Money decisions based on this robotic stimulus-induced response will never *feel* good.

Have you ever been caught up in purchasing platforms or working with a particular person because everyone around you seemed to be doing so, even if you were pretty sure you couldn't afford it? I know many entrepreneurs who are now employees for other businesses because this urge to robotically spend drove them into huge credit card debt that they simply couldn't afford. They had no specific return on investment to track against and the belief that one more program would be the trick to finally finding success actually sustained them right into bankruptcy.

Stories like that break my heart. Not just because I know they could have been successful with a little more balance in their money habits and alignment with their business stage, but because I know that had they listened to their internal voice a little more instead of having a robotic, external reaction, they would have felt much stronger and more confident in their financial decisions. Too often we disregard our internal voice of restraint in favor of external pressures and it can lead to financial disaster.

Now, I don't mean to say that a good business person will never be in debt. It's very hard to build a business without being upside down at some point, usually in the beginning, and later by design to take advantage of "good debt." But if you can generate your first, small successes without overwhelming your business with unsustainable expenses, you're much more likely to enjoy continued growth. How do you do that and conquer *bear brain* at the same time? Or better still, what do you do if you've gotten to an uncomfortable place around spending and want to turn it around? You put a plan in place.

I have an exercise that has successfully dealt with FOMO for many of my clients, and I suggest you try it is well. Bonus: It

ties into the "B" word we all love so much! (Hint: it's "budget.")
What if you were to allocate a certain amount of your resources
to your "I need it *now* because everyone else is doing it!" urges?
I ask my clients to map out which "extra" expenses (above-and-
beyond the "keeping-the-lights-on" costs) that they would like
to have in the next year. It might be attending an event or finally
purchasing an expensive CRM system. We make a budget for
these kinds of expenses and then they go into the year knowing
what they have to play with in their spending. If they spend
all that allocation in the first six months, then they commit
to not taking on anything new in this area without generating
significant additional income to cover it. The robotic external
response is quelled by the internally-driven voice and we can
not only establish healthy spending habits but feel completely
empowered in the process.

Let me give you an example of how to change your gut
buying response with a little math clarity. Look at that next
event you're dying to attend and determine how many new
clients or additional revenue you'd need to cover the costs.
For example, if you're a coach who sells a $2,800 program,
then a $10,000 mastermind opportunity that seems to be
the key to cracking your business wide open requires you to
sign five new clients to cover the cost of the mastermind plus
30 percent for taxes on the income, with a smidge left over
($2,800x5=$14,000; $10,000 for the cost of the program,
$3,000 tax set-aside, and just a bit extra for your operational
expenses). The problem with this example is that there's
nothing left over for *you* or to help cover the baseline costs of

your business. If you can't clearly see 1) the income potential you need to cover the costs, and 2) need to be able to take money out of your business to fund your personal life, then you might want to consider whether there's a way to garner those five clients in a different way. Perhaps the mastermind is something you can plan for next year, instead.

I recommend you try this approach when looking at your expenses within your business and start to get caught up in the excitement of the next program or "*I need it now*!" opportunity. (Sidebar: I keep hearing Veruca Salt's voice from the classic version of *Charlie and the Chocolate Factory* with Gene Wilder in my head while I write this. Try it yourself... it's a great way to identify *bear brain* around unsustainable spending and put in its proper place!)

## REFLECTION QUESTIONS

1. What kind of CEO are you now and what kind do you want to be in the future? How will you implement any changes you'd like to see?

2. How does looking at your biz numbers make you feel and where do you feel it?

3. What surprised you from looking at your financial statements?

4. Where can you make easy tweaks to shift your bottom line? What seems necessary but feels difficult to manage?

5. Are you making robotic (externally-driven) decisions or human (internally-driven) ones?

## EXERCISE
# Opening to Money

As we discussed in the last chapter, part of finding our *Zen* with money is getting comfortable receiving it. This can be *really* difficult for many of us. We all have various reasons that make it difficult to accept help – especially around finances. This can translate into how we perceive our value when pricing our services, or cause angst when it comes to asking for payment. To close out this chapter, let's look at your habits around receiving. Ask yourself these questions and write down your answers:

1. Is it hard to ask people for money? Find an example or two.
2. What happens when you need to price your services? How does it feel?
3. Are any of your old money stories coming up when you think about receiving money from clients?
4. Do you feel comfortable getting paid for your work? If so, are you crystal clear on how to set that up to your advantage? If not, what do you think is holding you back?
5. What would it feel like to receive money effortlessly? What would that look like for you? What would it take for it to feel that way?

## Bottom Line

Many of us struggle to get cozy and comfortable with our business finances. Misunderstanding the language and feeling insecure about our money decisions causes a great deal of discomfort and even panic. The best way I know to alleviate that is to move past the "Eek!" and look at your numbers to see what they're telling you. There's a story there, I promise, and it's not all bad, despite what you may be telling yourself.

If you want to find your financial balance, starting with the Right Speech – thoughtful communication to avoid dissention – is key, and you can start it right now by agreeing to interact with your finances in your businesses more regularly and with greater clarity around your ultimate goals. Once you've achieved a level of understanding about what you're earning and spending, and how much is left over for *you*, you'll feel better and your financial approach can become more balanced.

Chapter 5

# The Right Action

*"The best way to predict your future is to create it."*
**~ Abraham Lincoln**

I won't lie. I love being an entrepreneur. The flexibility and earning potential is lovely, of course, but being master of my own destiny on a day-to-day basis is paramount for me, as it is for a lot of people I know. Having entered the business owner game in a multi-person partnership, being accountable to no one but my clients and myself feels luxurious. It's why so many people get into entrepreneurship, whether they're tired of the nine-to-five and are adventurous enough to do something about it, or they're born with creative ideas brimming from the get-go.

These days the barrier to jumping in the pool is basically non-existent; with $5 on your credit card and a little initiative, you're up and running in our current online environment. There seem to be endless opportunities to dip your toe in and give it a whirl, particularly given that we can work with people all over the world with just a click of a button. Given this ease of entry to entrepreneurship, it's no surprise that many people who dream of a better life are beginning their own businesses, either part time or all-in right off the bat, with big dreams of easy hours and a healthy payout. And, frankly, why not? The water's fine in here!

One of the things that hangs many of us up when we first start making some money through our ventures, though, is how to take care of both our business *and* our personal lives at the same time. Managing our money can get tricky. So, now that we've peeked into handling our business finances, let's look at how to put our entrepreneurial efforts to work funding our personal lives. I like to call it the "Entrepreneurial Jackpot." When things are running smoothly in our personal finances, we're that much closer to finding our *Zen Money* and truly building the life of our dreams. And to accomplish it well, to live in financial integrity in our business *and* our personal lives, requires sticking to a few basic rules.

The primary tenet of the Right Action is encapsulated as acting in integrity, and generally approaching life via the lens of "do no wrong:" Refrain from stealing, develop a character that is self-controlled and mindful of others. It's as simple as that – a holistic approach to your environment that encourages you to act with integrity whenever possible to "safeguard the world for future generations." The vast majority of people I've met in my life inherently want that for themselves. Oddly enough, however, it can be difficult to master around our finances, particularly our personal money habits.

Instead we're often out of integrity with our finances, we spend more than we earn and are drowning in debt, aren't saving for retirement, or we're creating some other version of lack in our lives. These issues are very similar to how we approach money in our business, because we may not have been taught to handle it in a different way. It's not on purpose. We certainly don't intend to add stress and strain to our lives, our relationships, and our futures, but it happens again and again.

The question is: Now that we know how to put our money to work for us in our business, how do we translate those earnings to cash in our pockets, and how do we then build the life of our dreams?

## Building Your Bridge

In the last chapter, we discussed how to know if you're making money or not by paying attention to your bottom line: your net profit from your Profit & Loss Statement. It's time to talk about what everyone wants to know most: *How on earth do I support myself as an entrepreneur?*

Let's go back to our buckets of water exercise, and assume we're going to take all the water that's left in the business bucket and transfer it into our personal bucket, leaving nothing in the business for additional growth. Every month you have a choice with this, depending on your goals. Sometimes you might choose to leave more cash in the business to have on hand for a new opportunity (an event you'd like to attend, a new laptop you need to replace the one you drove over last week, to build up a cash reserve against future slowdowns, or any number of other unexpected business expenses outside of your standard costs). Other times, you'll want to (or need to), take it all out of the business for your personal use. In this case, let's assume that we're taking all of available our profit out of the business as an owner's draw. All the left-over, bottom-line water from our business bucket fills our personal bucket to the brim. This is going to be easy, because we can go through the *exact* same process as before, except we don't need to account for taxes because we've already done that part. Yippee!

Sidebar: Many people feel "taxes" is a dirty word and will do anything to avoid paying them, even to the point of ignoring them completely. (I don't recommend it.) I look at paying taxes a little differently; I see it as a privilege. When we're business owners, and we've lost the easy complaisance of regular employment where our taxes are automatically handled for us by our employers, it can feel tremendously burdensome to have to deal with the various levels of taxes. So why do I call it a privilege? Because if we owe taxes, it means we're making money! Consider that the next time you run up against a negative response to the word "taxes" and see if you can write a new positive story about your entrepreneurial success.

Okay, where were we? Right … we're looking at the water in our personal bucket and it's now time to give it jobs to do. You pour some out for fixed living expenses (mortgage, rent, car insurance, school loans) and now you're down to half of your bucket filled. It's starting to feel a little tight when you pour out more for food and dance classes for your kids and plane tickets and hotel for the family wedding you're all attending next summer. Once you're done pouring out water for these things, there's not much left in your bucket, and you're starting to feel demoralized. How on earth do we manage to give back to our community, build our dream life, and feel abundant around it all? If you're like many entrepreneurs I know, this is the exact question keeping you up at night, feeling panicky (hello, *bear brain*, there you are again!).

Let's dive into it by looking at a little more math....

## The Financial Equation Redux

The basic financial equation is a closed environment. What do I mean by that? We can only work with what we have on hand, starting with your income. If we have more expenses than income, then we're upside down (a.k.a. in the red, taking a loss, losing money). That may be okay occasionally, but your goal should always be to have more to play with rather than less on a regular basis. It's how you grow, build a cushion, save for retirement, and other financial goals you outlined in the exercises in Chapter Two.

What does this mean for our personal finances? It means that if our income is limited, so is our ability to spend ... or it should be. Unfortunately, in today's easy-credit environment, many of us are carrying debt *and* trying to live an abundant lifestyle. The advertising companies tell us it's possible, but the reality is that we can't get around the math without putting ourselves in financial jeopardy.

But don't let that financial fear grow out of control just yet. There are ways to get a handle on your debt and still live your life. It just means understanding your financial equation and working with what you have in your personal bucket to accomplish it. We'll talk more about debt in later chapters, but for now, let's resume our look at your current personal finances.

Once you have a clear picture of your money reality, you'll be able to put a coherent plan in place to manage it.

## Your Personal P&L

Did you know you could create a Profit & Loss Statement from your personal finances just as you can in your business? It's a great tool in thinking about and managing your money. The math is just the same: Income - Expenses = Profit. In this case, I would define "profit" to be "what's left over to play with." Just as we allocated a certain amount to taxes on the business side, you can allocate certain amounts to non-essential things in your life. For one person, that might mean saving for travel, for another it might mean making charitable donations.

The main goal right now is to build your personal P&L so you can see how much is on your bottom line to utilize. You can do this by hand and simply start with the cash you plan to take out of your business and subtract out your regular living costs first, followed by unusual expenses that you know crop up from time to time, or you can use a spreadsheet or a fancy personal finance tracking program. Whatever's left over after you've taken cash out of your business and subtracted out your living expenses is your "dream money," the amount on a monthly basis you have to allocate to doing things that fulfill you.

Remember how you created your personal and relationship goals? This is a great time to get those out and review your actual financial situation against those hopes and dreams. Do any of the parameters need to change? Perhaps it'll take a little longer to meet some of your goals because there's less money available than you thought. Or perhaps you'll realize you have more on hand than you expected, and you can move up your deadlines.

Or the one I like the most: Perhaps seeing the numbers written down in black and white will solidify your resolve to simply make more money in your business, so you have a bigger bucket to work with in your personal life. The easiest way to have more money on hand is to create more income, hands down! So, if you're feeling strapped for cash, even if business is booming and growing soundly, figuring out how to generate additional revenue is the name of the game. Just keep in mind that any additional income will not directly translate into cash in pocket. You need to account for taxes and any additional expenses you take on in the business to generate the new income.

All of this can feel overwhelming when you're used to taking home a regular paycheck. The financial ups and downs of a new business can be hair-raising when you're trying to live the same lifestyle as you did as an employee. Our goal is to vastly surpass that income, but in the beginning, we might need to change some of our money habits to be successful long-term.

## Paying Yourself First

Okay, I'm guessing you've heard this phrase before. It's popular in entrepreneurial circles based on the simple reality that if we don't put a plan in place for our business to pay us, it won't happen. It's the same principle at work as the one that keeps your front porch from getting painted because it's listed under the "someday" column of your to-do list. In the game of giving our money a job to do, if we leave out putting cash in our own pocket, the business will inevitably eat up any available cash. It's weird, but true, and putting a plan in place that includes paying yourself will alleviate any confusion or discontent that comes from never having any cash on hand for our personal lives.

And I'm guessing that while you're excited about helping clients and all, you're working really hard to also pay the mortgage, put food on your table, and maybe send your kids to college and yourself on a vacation once in a while, right? So how do we make sure you have enough money to take out for your own use? We *plan* for it!

Let's look at this in detail. Remember, for our business to be healthy, we need to earn more than we spend. What if we build our take-home pay into our business calculations (again, this is what's called an owner's draw or distribution, and not traditional employee-style payroll, at least in the beginning of our business growth)? If you plan on taking cash out every month, then you can work your income requirements backward to figure out what your revenue target needs to be. In the last chapter, we used an example of how to use bottom-up pricing to determine our fees. That example is perfect for talking about how to pay yourself first. Let's say you earn $12,500, set aside $3,750 (30 percent) for taxes, and plan to take $5,000 out for yourself. That leaves you $3,750 for business expenses. This is how we can work the math for paying yourself first. If your business can't survive on the $3,750 that you've allocated for expenses, you'll need to adjust your take-home expectations.

Now, what do we do if we don't have the cash on hand to cover our personal needs, even if we've earned enough to do so? Sometimes it takes a while for our cash to catch up, especially if you offer your clients payment terms. This issue can have a serious impact on our personal cash flow, just as it does in our business. Ideally, this where we need to be a little flexible, and perhaps work on building our cash buffer up a bit in our business before we ramp up to taking our full "salary" amount. You need to ask yourself whether it's more comfortable to build the business platform fully – including a cash buffer that allows the money to flow easily – before taking your ideal take-home pay, or whether you want to continue playing the shell game with your cash as your business grows.

It you have a plan for paying yourself, it allows you to see where you can make adjustments in your business spending, or your pricing – *or both* – that allow you to hit your money goals (and achieve that feeling of *Zen Money*) sooner than later. Are you currently taking money out haphazardly? Look at your numbers for the past several months and put a plan in place that allows you to include paying yourself in the process, without robbing from your future business needs. If you happen to be in the enviable position of not needing to pay yourself out of your business, I also recommend making a point of paying yourself a small amount each month anyway, to get in the habit of planning for it. That way, you won't forget to include your take-home when you *are* ready to start paying yourself for your efforts. Even $20/month will embed the habit.

## The Spending Game

Let's dive a little deeper into why so many of us are tied up in knots about our personal finances and the best way I know to relieve that anxiety. Have you ever felt a surge of adrenaline when you're out shopping? For some people, it can be addicting. That powerful feeling, combined with a disconnected understanding of finance, can be a recipe for disaster.

Unfortunately, in this day and age, too many people are completely strapped financially because of overspending. It's insidious when you can take a step back and look at our habits as a culture with a clear eye. Mortgage companies still love to put people in houses beyond their means, making them "house poor" and thereby creating a downward spiral in not only our credit scores but, equally important, in our emotional well-being. I don't know about you, but I experienced that kind of financially limited existence in my twenties (credit cards, not mortgages) and I found it incredibly uncomfortable. It's a limiting way to live, and not being in that space is the exact opposite: exhilarating!

I can hear you think "But Liz, that's all fine and good, but how do I fix it?" There are two things that need to happen for you to reach financial nirvana around your spending: paying attention and making a plan. If you're in the habit of throwing down your credit card without a thought, then it's time for an exercise I like to call "Get in the Flow." It's really simple. All you have to do is start watching how money is coming in and out of your life. Seems simple right? It's actually not. It's very easy to slip into *shoulding* ourselves when we start to pay attention, which frankly isn't very productive. The key here is to just pay attention to the flow of money coming in and going out. You can do it in your business and your personal life, preferably over a week or more to really see the rhythms in your "money breath" – both in and out. Let yourself be wildly curious, and, like an explorer in your own home, document your findings. So often we simply buy because we want something in the moment, without much in the way of long-term benefit, and this is a great way to begin making a connection between your outflow and your actual needs.

Once we break the habitual cycles, it's easy to make alternative financial choices and give our money different jobs to do. I had a client who habitually hit the Dunkin' Donuts drive-through every day on her way to drop her kids at school. Once she started looking at her financial flow (remember: where we place our attention grows), she realized she was spending nearly $400/month on coffee and treats! When that became clear, it was incredibly easy to change her habits and allocate the majority of that money to a different project (in her case, saving for a family vacation). She allowed herself a couple of coffee stops a month instead and never felt any lack around the decision. She actually felt empowered because she could truly enjoy those special coffee days *and* feel financial confident all at the same time.

What spending habits might be lurking in your life that you could put to better use? Take a week and pay attention, then, if you don't like what you see, make a plan to give your money a different job – one that *feels* more in alignment with your bigger life dreams. It can be a liberating experience!

## Love & Money

The hardest part about entrepreneurship, in my opinion, is navigating the rough waters of relationships. You're highly focused and deeply interested in growing your business, which takes a massive amount of your attention – energy you might previously have bestowed upon a loved one. So, you're already under the gun in terms of time and attention, and you may now find yourself with another layer of uncomfortable conversations around money. It's especially hard if you're not sure how much you can pay yourself out of your business; it makes it hard to have a productive and non-combative conversation about family finances.

If you're in a long-term partnership or marriage, you know all about the balance beam between your partner's loving, proud support of your entrepreneurial adventure and plain ol' discomfort when they see money funneling out the door with *nada* coming in. Couples in general have a hard time getting on the same page around their finances, and then when we throw entrepreneurial uncertainty into the mix, it can get quite uncomfortable for both parties. Left untended, these issues can create long-lasting scars in your relationship, your own sense of self-worth, and possible consequences as your children witness your skirmishes while you and your partner dance around your fear and pain over your finances.

I'm not a relationship coach, so I'd like to talk about this issue through the lens of … you guessed it… the numbers! As you now well know, I'm a firm believer that looking at the numbers is the best place to start if you want to peel back the layers of your financial discomfort. If your earning or spending within your business is a source of pain in your personal relationships, then the work you did in the last chapter will help. The better you understand what's going on in your business, the more confidently and competently you can have open discussions with your loved one(s).

I've had several clients who are the sole bread-winners for their families struggle to talk about their business finances, their plans and big dreams, in a way that didn't cause an argument with their spouse. Most of the time, it stemmed from them not being able to clearly articulate their vision for the business and how they saw it funding their goals for their families. Often, as entrepreneurs, we're dreaming on multiple levels, aren't we? If we can get ten extra clients, then we can hire an assistant *and* take out more money, which means we can buy the new car we need or pay down the mortgage faster or send Sally to summer camp in California this year. Our dreams move and shift rapidly, especially when things are starting to gain traction, and it can be hard for our spouses to keep up. And, of course, if you're anything like me, you forget that your partner doesn't hear what's going on inside your head, so they're feeling more left out than you might realize. (I thought I told you that. Didn't I tell you that? I definitely *meant* to tell you that.)

When our income is uneven, especially in the beginning and without a clear plan in place, it can be terrifying for our loved ones. When I first started my business, my husband was massively uncomfortable about the fact that money wasn't coming in and he worried that the money I was using to build the business (payout from the sale of my shares of another partnership) was being pumped down the drain. He couldn't see the intrinsic investment value I could, because he didn't live in my body and know to his core that I could make this thing fly. It took a solid year and my being able to begin regularly contributions to our household expenses again before he started breathing easier. And because I purposely made sure the business was well-established financially before I began drawing money out, it was perhaps more prolonged an agony than it needed to be. And, of course, *I* needed the security of knowing the biz was viable and had solidly graduated to Business Adult before I started taking a paycheck, so that added to the stress on both sides.

I won't lie, I totally resented him for his discomfort. I felt like he didn't have faith in my abilities. In hindsight, it makes sense that he felt like he was on a roller-coaster with a blindfold on … he basically was when I didn't share what was happening. Now I recognize that his own financial stories were torturing him, and I've learned to share more about what's going on in the business, so he can feel like a participant and not just a helpless bystander. It's a fine line, of course, because sometimes knowing the intimate financial details can cause your partner to either 1) Question all your choices, which as a non-entrepreneur may seem radical because he/she has a lower risk tolerance than you do, and/or 2) Strip you of feelings of independence and pride in the Business Baby you're lovingly nurturing.

Whatever your situation, I would recommend going back to our standby of "pay attention and make a plan." Knowing your business numbers so you're aware of how much you can add to your personal coffers is a great place to start. Keying into your partner's feelings around money and your entrepreneurial journey and giving them the gift of developing a plan together for your personal life is the next part. A little information about your combined financial picture can go a long way toward alleviating strain in your relationships. Putting an actionable plan in place can help alleviate any sense of helplessness your loved one(s) may be feeling and afford you the opportunity to fully step into your role as CEO of your business, armed with data and ready for action.

## Bear Brain: I Can Afford It!

One of the ways *bear brain* can show up when we start to take control of our personal finances, especially when our business is just ramping up, comes in the form of excitement that leads to excess. Now, perhaps that's a dirty word to use, but there's a fine line between celebrating our successes and spending beyond our means. Since I know you're here because you have a big mission and big goals for your business, yourself, and your community, it's important to take a hard look at where our ego might show up when we start making money, and how we keep it from sabotaging our hard-earned financial gains.

It's easy in our entrepreneurial excitement to blow right past the Business Teenager stage when the money starts coming in. We think we can afford everything, and once we get a handle on how to earn money, we tell ourselves, "No big deal, I'll make up the difference with a few more sales." Except when that money comes in, maybe we don't set aside for taxes and we find something else we can't live without, further complicating our financial picture.

I have a client who consistently journaled, "I can buy anything I want," for several months. Guess what? She broke earning records in her business, rode the high, and manifested her wish. She spent to her heart's content, not realizing that she was undermining other financial desires she had: building a cushion of cash and paying down personal debt. When she realized what was happening, she quickly changed her habits and now has a plan in place to take care of the business first and work on her other, less fun, personal goals, while curtailing her free-for-all spending. Now she writes a daily intention that reads, "I have $10,000 in all of my accounts." I imagine once she achieves that goal, it will shift again to a new, bigger vision.

This story isn't meant to shame you. If you're making money and are excited about it and want to celebrate, I get it. I want to celebrate with you! I'd love if you could take a minute and be wildly curious, though, and determine what kind of job you could give your new resources that would feel the best, for the longest, so that this version of *bear brain* doesn't get the best of you. Because I have to say, long-term money goals like paying off a mortgage are sweet when they're achieved. Much longer lasting a high than a trip to the mall. So, what's the solution? You guessed it! Let's make a plan that includes you being able to celebrate and still work on those other goals you might have. And watch your language around it, too. You just might get exactly what you ask for.

## REFLECTION QUESTIONS

1. What does the math of your financial bridge tell you? Is it different than you thought?

2. How does your personal financial reality make you feel and where do you feel it (your gut, your heart, elsewhere)?

3. What do you observe when you're wildly curious about how money flows in your life?

4. Where can you make easy tweaks to shift your personal bottom line? What seems necessary but feels difficult to manage?

5. Are you struggling to manage your Entrepreneurial Journey with a loved one? What are some ways you might change the conversation?

6. How is an excited *bear brain* showing up for you and what can you do to combat it?

## EXERCISE
# Fall in LOVE

Let's redefine our relationship with our cash! While we're talking about your spending habits, let's also take some time to make an emotional shift. For the next seven days, I want you to write a love letter to your money. It can be a short note, a long epistle, whatever comes up for you on that day. Think about what you're grateful for in terms of your money and put that gratitude on paper. You can even post your notes in your office or on your fridge as lovely reminders of the positive ways money is working in your life.

Start them *"Dear Money..."* and go where your heart takes you! I've led this exercise with clients to great success. Even if you're feeling like your relationship with money is on solid footing, I encourage you to commit to it for the next week. The simple act of physically writing the notes can create a new awareness about our habits and allow us to adjust old patterns to fit our new reality.

---
## EXERCISE
# Personal and Community Goals

It's time for a reset! If you've been diligently pondering the concepts and doing the activities so far, you should get a great deal out of this one. Take ten minutes and free-write about your personal and community financial goals. These may be the same ones you came up with in the financial clarity exercise in Chapter Two or they may be different (or additions). Note any new ideas or expanded thoughts as you dream up your perfect money reality for your life. Where are you living? What are you doing? Who are you with? Are you giving to charity? Which one? Are you funding a big mission?

The purpose of this exercise is to remind you of your *why*. We've delved into a lot of nitty-gritty processing here, and I want to be sure we're moving away from the "ick" and toward your vision in a way that continues to *feel* great.

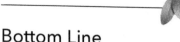

## Bottom Line

Our Entrepreneurial Adventure can wreak havoc in our personal finances, particularly when we're first figuring out how to pay ourselves consistently and well. It can be tempting to grab all the cash available in the business to level-up our personal life in tandem with our growing success. I absolutely want you to be able to celebrate your achievements and enjoy some newfound freedom around your finances. It's hard living on the edge, which many of us do while we're ramping up our business and it's oh-so-tempting to let off a little money steam to relieve the pressures we feel from our relationships, our own expectations of ourselves, and our vision for life as an entrepreneur.

A great way to navigate that morass effectively is by watching your habits with money and consciously changing anything that no longer serves you. Paying attention and making a plan are the bedrock of the Right Action to creating your version of *Zen Money*. I think you'll find that getting comfortably familiar with your patterns and financial realities will go a long way toward changing your personal financial outlook and put you firmly on the path to reaching your big money visions … sooner than you may expect.

## Chapter 6

# The Right Livelihood

*"Excellence is an art won by training and habit. We do not act rightly because we have virtue or excellence, but we rather have those because we have acted rightly. We are what we repeatedly do. Excellence, then, is not an act but a habit."*

**~ Aristotle**

Sunday mornings at my house include paying our kids their weekly allowance. We started this money ritual when my son turned five. If they completed a few, easy chores around the house throughout the week, they could put two dollars in their piggy banks. As they've grown, the complexity and number of jobs has increased (although the payment has yet to, skinflints that we are). The first step in teaching our kids good money habits is the actual earning of the cash, and the next piece involves rules around how they use it. We require them to put half of their earnings in the bank, and they can spend whatever is left over on special treats (usually Legos and books). They also contribute to (or cover entirely) holiday and birthday gifts for each other and close family members.

Do you know what I've learned from watching my children handle their money from these weekly experiences? We all have an inherent approach to money. My son is a spender while my daughter is a hoarder. My daughter clearly feels her needs are met and often will decline the opportunity to spend her money. At one point we counted her stash, and she was sitting on $180 in fives and ones squirreled around her room. She's actually *lost* her money in our house twice, because while she doesn't spend it, she also doesn't pay much attention to it.

In an interesting twist, my son knows down to the penny how much he has on hand, and how much needs to go into his savings account should he ask to purchase a new Star Wars Lego kit. He is constantly short on funds, but he is actively in the money flow, giving it jobs to do as soon as he receives his allowance. So which version is better? I've come to believe that both approaches work, with a little clarity and structure in their habits. For my son, we've encouraged him to set money goals that include other opportunities than simply adding to the mountain of small plastic bricks littering our floors. For my daughter, we've established a "track it or lose it" policy and she knows that if she misplaces her funds again and we find it, we get to keep the money. I've also started asking her what she's saving it for, so she can start thinking about what kinds of jobs to give her ducats instead of leaving them languishing on her bureau.

Both are learning how to handle their money from a young age. We're attempting to remove the mystery of how it works so they can develop solid financial habits now instead of floundering as a young adult, as many do. This idea of building rituals around your finances is as important for your financial success as it is for my kids.

Our *Zen* tenet for the Right Livelihood is this: Your work must have a respect for life, and your work must reflect it. How does that translate to our financial world? I like to look at it through the prism of ritual. That means building consistent habits around your financial management – both in your business and out of it – and, in doing so, you build a healthy respect for your money. Your diligence will be reflected to you in peace of mind and the ability to make sound strategic decisions.

## Your Current Money Rituals

Let's take a few minutes and look at what's going on with your current financial rituals. If you think you don't have any, look again; we all have habits when it comes to our money. The question is: Are you utilizing these habits consciously to your best benefit or not? At this point, you're likely feeling more on top of what's happening around your money. However, I'm guessing that some of your rituals are working well and some of your money habits aren't as helpful as they might be. But we won't know until we take a look at them.

Our goal is to build ourselves a few beautiful new rituals that feel spectacular and allow us to continue to establish a much more loving, positive relationship with money than we've had in the past. Think of it as an energetic exchange: If we use money inconsistently or without a framework for managing it (i.e. good money habits), then we're all over the place, taking on too much and not getting value for our efforts.

With money rituals that *feel* good, we can begin to see what's happening in our lives around our finances and start to see a consistent, even flow, rather than ups and downs that feel out of our control and disruptive. It's not unlike developing a healthier eating habit or getting in the groove with an exercise routine that takes you to the next level of fitness. In the beginning, it can feel arduous and we may want to give up. What do you do to push through besides reminding yourself of your goal (which is a great way to stay on track, too)? The most successful habit-building includes elements of fun! So, I want you to consider how to turn that millstone vibe around your money work into the endorphin high of a good, sweaty workout.

What exactly might a money ritual look like? Some people take their money on a date. They carve out a time once a week to look at their money and create ways to make it enjoyable. Perhaps you sit down with a nice cup of tea and a little bit of chocolate, follow up on unpaid invoices, and check your bookkeeping. Maybe you have "sushi-and-statements" Mondays, to entice yourself to create a habit of looking at your money regularly. Even half an hour a week dedicated to looking at your income and your expenses, in your business and your personal life, can go a *long* way toward feeling in control with your finances (not to mention getting cash in hand faster when you're looking at what invoices are still outstanding).

Part of the way that we can make this a lot more fun is to develop a ritual that feels great. It might be including something delicious to eat, that you can enjoy while you're doing your financial work. Maybe you put on music that really energizes you, or is kind of mellow, depending on what mood you want to be in when you're working with your numbers.

I have clients who were well aware they were hiding from their numbers, even though they *knew* what they had to do to stay on top of their finances and even believed it wasn't particularly difficult to manage. They just had "fallen off the wagon" and the idea of getting back to a regular, weekly check-in had started feeling like a big old *should*. When I suggested taking their money on a date, they were able to get re-energized around this part of their business and started enjoying their weekly quiet time with their numbers.

So, think about how you want to feel when you're doing your important financial work. My guess is, historically you haven't felt awesome about doing it, or it's just been an annoying task that you check off your list. What if you can flip that internal story and make your regular financial work – invoicing, paying bills, checking statements, and reading reports – really juicy and fun, so that you want to do this work on a regular basis and continue to feel empowered? With a good money ritual, you can consistently feel on top of the world when you're looking at your numbers.

## Relationship Rituals

In the last chapter, we started the conversation about how to develop a positive conversation around money with your partner. That relationship is a fantastic place to implement a new ritual or two around money. It can be a turning point in moving from angst to awesome, as you open financial discussions to include your partner or other loved ones. Do you currently have any habits you might be unaware of in this area? Perhaps you both consistently avoid looking at your financial statements – separately or together. That's a habit. Perhaps you fight over your low bank balances or blame the other for being unable to reach your family's financial goals. Those are also habits.

Our goal in looking at your relationship rituals is to identify areas that aren't serving you any longer (typically in the form of hiding or fighting) and replace them with rituals that establish greater intimacy and connection with your loved one. How do we do it? We pay attention and we make a plan ... of course!

I have a friend who established a very positive monthly ritual with her husband several years ago. They have a busy lifestyle, with two active daughters and a great deal of work-related travel, so they were often feeling caught short around their finances, mostly because they didn't ever seem to be in the same place at the same time to get on the same financial page. They wanted that very much, but the lack of communication about their finances and their money goals was starting to take a toll. So, they established a new routine.

Now, they sit down together and have a date night with their money, once a month. They set out a nice bottle of wine with glasses on the ready, knowing that once they're done with the financial work (which they've both agreed is very important for the wellbeing and upkeep of their household, as well as their personal relationship), they can enjoy a glass of wine together. They review her take-home projects for her business, their family spending against a budget, and then they look at what's coming down the pike. They also look at their schedules and talk about any out-of-the-norm expenses that might be coming up for them as a family (ski season starting with new equipment purchases, family vacation in a few months with plane tickets to be bought, etc.). They have a lovely evening with just the two of them, where they're able to talk about their lives in an open way they had missed once the busy details of life took away opportunities to just sit together and dream. And all through the management of their money!

I truly believe that creating good financial habits is about more than simply knowing your numbers. It can and should catalyze bigger conversations: "Where do we want to go in our life together?" Not just "Oh my god, we have to put money aside for the roof!" but also, "Hey, let's dream a little about where we want to take the kids on vacation," and "How can I really use my money so that I'm feeling abundant, and open, and not having to work so hard?" And the beauty of shifting into this approach is that you can do it for yourself, whether you're in a relationship or not.

Given this conversation around money rituals, and considering all the pieces of your money puzzle that you may want to be paying more attention to than you are currently, how can you do it in a way that feels luxurious, beautiful, and like something that you'll want to do on a regular basis? What rituals sing to you the most? What would make this process of looking at your numbers *feel* good?

## Fantastic Financial Habits

You know when you get into a rhythm and everything feels great around that part of your life? You've got your morning routine that helps you greet the day with enthusiasm, and an evening routine that helps you slip into a lovely, deep sleep. As entrepreneurs, we learn to rely on healthy practices to keep our engines running at optimal levels, so we can continue growing. Developing great financial habits is no different. In my mind, the goal isn't to stay on track with your invoices, bills, and looking at your financial reports because we're *supposed* to. The goal is to develop a desire to do this work well because it makes you *feel* amazing when all aspects of your financial world are humming along easily for you.

The second part of developing our money rituals requires a look at how we're interacting with our money daily, both within and outside of our business. As I'm sure you're aware, there are financial activities that need to happen for any business to be successful: sending invoices, making sure we get paid, paying our bills on time, and spending to our advantage. I wrote about a lot of the how-to "ticky tacky" around your financial habits in *From Zero to Zen*. Right now, I want to talk about how to build new, CEO-oriented habits to your advantage.

Let's assume for now that your bookkeeping is at least mostly on track, that you've got a client-onboarding process that gets you paid quickly and easily, and that you're taking care of your bills and taxes. Many entrepreneurs I know ask, "What else do I need to be doing? I'm all set, right?" My answer: yes and no. Taking care of your daily, weekly, monthly, quarterly, and annual financial tasks is absolutely the first and most important step. But it's not just about doing this work – or having it done for you. The bigger question you need to ask yourself is *why* are we doing the work? And the answer is: We track our numbers so we can use them to our advantage!

How do we do that? We start by getting intimately familiar with our financial reports in our business and learn to understand at a glance what they're telling us. So many smart, savvy entrepreneurs I know don't look at their Profit & Loss Statement or Balance Sheet regularly and may not even check their cash balances that often. Others are intimately aware of how much is in their checking account, but they can't say whether they've made any profit in the past 30 days. This is where you can truly set yourself apart from the competition.

All it takes is a commitment to looking at your three main financial reports on a regular basis. I'm not kidding here, it really is that easy, if we let ourselves get past the discomfort around the idea. What are these reports again? They're your:

- Profit & Loss Statement (a.k.a. P&L or Income Statement) – This report shows your income and expenses in a certain period of time and is based on our primary financial equation (Income – Expenses = Profit).

- Balance Sheet – This report gives you a point-in-time view of the health of your business, looking at what you have of value, what you owe other people, and what's left over (Assets – Liabilities = Equity).

- Statement of Cash Flow – This third report shows you how much cash you brought in and how much you've spent in any given period. It's a great addition to the first two, because it helps you identify where your money is going in real time. (More on using cash flow to your advantage in the next chapter.)

I want you to be familiar with these three reports, because if you regularly pay attention to what they're telling you, they can catalyze your financial growth like nothing else. If you're taking care of your own books and using software that automatically generates these reports for you, fantastic! Look at them at least once a month, after you've reconciled your bank statements. If you work with a bookkeeper, they should be sending these to you consistently (hopefully within 10-15 days after closing out the prior month).

This is where the rubber hits the road in your ability to up-level your entrepreneurial game, and the reason we're doing all this tracking in the first place. Remember when I said that information is key? The information you need to know if you're making money, if you can afford to pay yourself, and how to tweak your numbers to your advantage lives in these reports. If you had a magic mirror to ask about your future, you'd likely use it, right? So why aren't you taking advantage of your financial crystal ball in your business? That's what you give up when you don't look at your reports regularly.

So, make your financial review a priority. When you take your money on a date, don't forget to bring along your reports and get really intimate with them. It's the easiest way I know for you step fully into your role as expert CEO. Be prepared to look at your booked income and your cash flow (not necessarily the same thing … more on this in Chapter Eight). Set aside time to review any changes in the value of your business when you check in on your Balance Sheet.

On the personal side, you can do the same thing. In fact, I like to look at my business numbers and track them against my personal numbers at the same time. The math works the same way, so it's an easy habit to develop and keep. After you review how well (or poorly) your business did in the previous month, look at what you brought home and where you spent it. Was there anything left over to play with? If so, what do you plan to do with it? How can you move all aspects of your life forward, using this information?

Asking yourself questions like these are all you need to start establishing fantastic financial habits within your business and your personal life. It's as simple as setting aside time once a month for a little exploration into what exactly your numbers tell you – not just doing the daily bookkeeping work because someone told you it needed to happen. This review can help you to stop hiding from your money reality and start living as the powerful business owner you are. Once you've made the decision to become this new version of yourself, all the *shoulding* melts away and you can simply build this numbers review work into your beautiful money rituals.

## Bear Brain: I DON'T LIKE THIS!

Okay, I'm sure it won't come as a surprise to you that *bear brain* around our money habits usually shows up as a temper tantrum. It's not unlike getting into the groove with a new exercise regime, when in the second week all you want to do is stay in bed instead of getting up and heading to the gym. It's so simple to let ourselves off the hook, but when we stick to our plans, we wind up feeling *amazing* afterward. Not only because we worked our muscles (financial or otherwise), but also because we stayed committed to ourselves and our big goals.

When building new financial habits, like anything, it's easy to start off well in the initial excitement but fall off the wagon within a month or two because we're distracted by new, shiny ideas and projects. Don't let that happen! Decide right now, in this moment, how you plan to combat the inevitable *bear brain* voice in your head telling you, "I don't like this! I don't understand it! Things are fine as they are!" Set yourself up for success by putting a reward system in place. Take yourself out for dinner after you've opened your credit card statement and looked at your financial reports next month. Ask a friend to hold you accountable. All the tricks you've used to create new habits in other areas of your life are applicable here. Once you determine that you *want* to be the person who knows her numbers, don't let *bear brain* get in the way by throwing a fit just as you're getting started!

## REFLECTION QUESTIONS

1. How will you fit your financial work into your schedule?
2. What might come up to sabotage you and how will you stay on track?
3. What rituals can you implement that make your money habits *feel* great?
4. Who's on your financial team now? In the future?

## EXERCISE
# Your Beautiful Money Ritual

In this exercise, I'd like you to take some time and consider what you could put into place to develop not just good money habits, but ones that feel *great*. For some people, that looks like a regular date, with a glass of wine or some chocolate while reviewing the numbers and recording details. For others, that might be simply carving out time for Money Mondays every week. If you have a spouse or partner, setting aside specific time to review the finances – one that's fun and engaging – can make a huge difference in both your comfort levels around your money.

What money rituals sing to you? Write down in detail what they look like, how often they'll happen, and how you think it will feel to establish this new pattern with your finances.

## Bottom Line

Like anything in our lives, developing habitual practices can quickly change from feeling onerous to something you look forward to. Have you ever changed your diet – let's say started drinking green smoothies – and in the beginning, you weren't sure it was for you, but over time and with repetition, your morning routine starts to feel empty without it? The same thing can happen with your financial rituals. I encourage you to explore what's been holding you back and how you might change that story for yourself.

We've talked a lot about paying attention to our numbers. It's equally important to pay attention to the financial rituals we're building up along the way, and the new money habits you want to create to ensure your success. Having rituals gives meaning to our actions, and requires a level of respect – for ourselves, for the work, and ultimately for our desired

## Chapter 7

# The Right Effort

*"In order to carry a positive action, we must develop here a positive vision."*

**~ Dalai Lama**

Have you ever pushed yourself *hard*, only to see mediocre results? The truth is, sometimes working harder isn't the answer. Many of the successful entrepreneurs I know have spent a great deal of time and money changing old habits to get better outcomes, in less time, and with less effort. And at the core of all of it is the ability to step back and take a bird's eye view of our situation. Successful financial management is no different.

The concept of the Right Effort is to develop your mind and limit distractions to further hone your practices, with clear and honest thoughts that leave a conflicted, muddled mind behind. In our financial work, I see this as cultivating positivity toward our money practices, without being overly black-and-white or excessively laissez-faire about our numbers management. We're looking for the Three Bears philosophy here: not too rigid and not too loosey-goosey … we want "just right!" Why do we care about developing the Right Effort? Doing so can put you well on your path to *Zen Money* and create an attitude of cheerful determination in the process.

This is your path to empowerment – when you take the information that you've started collecting in the past few chapters and start bringing it all together to work for you in your business, your personal life, and beyond. In doing so, you gain control of your finances in a way that is infinitely rewarding.

## The Sticking Point: Cash Flow 101

Okay, I can hear you thinking, "Liz, this is all well and good, but even if I know how to set my pricing, and understand my income and expenses, I never seem to have enough cash on hand." What exactly is going on when we find it hard to get over the "hump" in our businesses around cash flow? This is a term everyone likes to use but not many people really seem to understand. Cash flow, simply put, is the amount of money that goes in and out of your business in a given period of time. What can trip up a lot of new entrepreneurs is that while we may have a nice month on paper (booked income), depending on your payment terms, it might take a while for that cash to show up in our bank accounts. If we're continually spending right up to the limit, then you can easily fall into the shell game of moving money around without ever getting ahead.

So, how do we manage your cash flow to your advantage? It's very simple. Make a plan for your money *before* it comes in the door and stick to it when it does. The place we often get tripped up is around taxes. When cash flow is tight, as it often is as we're growing, it can be so easy to ignore the fact that we have to pay taxes on our earnings. The money comes in and our credit card is due, and we need to pay ourselves something to cover the mortgage, and that new program looks like a great idea, too. Suddenly, that nice fat bank balance is back down to nothing and you're scrambling again.

Managing cash flow well is as simple as referring to our basic financial equation again. I know, I know ... you're sick of it, but it can really save your neck if you let it. The bottom line in this version of the math is "Don't spend more cash than you have." Then keep doing that month after month, until you accrue a nice cushion in your business checking account. If you can do it in your personal life as well, you'll get the same results. And when those buffers are built, it's so much easier to say "Yes!" to that new training or to finally take that family vacation. Consider what's happening in your cash flow today and how you'd like to it be in the future. How much money hit your bank account last month, and how much went out? The month before that? Do you need to generate more income? Can you reduce expenses anywhere? Once you have a clear picture, you'll be able to start creating the extra monies I know will make you feel better by having on hand. It's the best way I know for money to easily flow from your business to your personal life and beyond. For some entrepreneurs, that might look like a cash buffer of three or six months' worth of expenses. Some people are most comfortable having a year of cash on hand. Part of our goal is to determine what level of cash comfort feels best for *you*.

It can be tricky in the beginning, especially when it feels like every part of your life is screaming for a money injection. The idea of building a buffer is limiting, if not daunting. You may need to scrimp and save for a while to set yourself up for success. I can promise you that the long-term benefits are incalculable, though. When the cash catches up, you'll find a financial freedom you can revel in. You'll no longer worry about saying "yes" to that expense you hadn't planned for and you'll be able to pivot when needed without putting your personal finances in jeopardy.

I look at this piece of your financial journey as similar to mine with Lyme disease. There are pieces of my daily life that aren't that much fun. If I want to go on vacation with my family, I need to eat really cleanly, manage my exercise and energy, and make sure I'm in tip-top shape so I can truly enjoy our time away together. That might mean zero sugar, early nights, and a tight management of my schedule, which sometimes feels very limiting. However, being able to revel in a trip with my family is nirvana for me, so these limitations are well worth it in the long run. If you've been playing the shell game with your business and/or personal finances, I encourage you to put an aggressive plan in place that will allow you the financial freedom you crave – even if it feels restrictive right now. I promise that your future self (and healthy business) will thank you for it!

## Who Is This For?

At this point in the game when I'm working with clients, many people start to glaze over. It's a lot to take in, and it's not always painless. We like to think, "Sweet! I know it now, I'm all set, right?" Except sound financial management is a life-long exercise. It's a marathon, and it's easy to want to give up just when we're hitting our stride. The best way I know to stay on track with our finances – even when we'd rather not stick to our new habits – is to remember why it's important. I'm guessing if you've hit six figures or beyond in your business, it's because you're dedicated. I'm also guessing there may be other reasons in your life that motivate you. That might be your family, or an aging parent, the desire to fund your retirement accounts, or build a movement.

Take a minute here and reflect on what you've learned so far. We're most likely to implement new ideas if they're intimately tied to our purpose. So, what's yours? Who are you working for and what will it mean if you get your finances humming? What will you do with the extra cash in your pocket and how will your business thrive with your financial attention? What makes doing the work worth your while?

## EXERCISE
## Your Money Story

While we're in reflection mode, let's take a minute to recap further. We've discussed building the bridge between your business and your personal life in a sustainable way, and how you can tell what's going on with your finances. Now it's story time. What exactly is your money telling you? If you're looking at your numbers regularly, and getting comfortable with them, you should start to see patterns emerge. It's very much like learning to read or ride a bike. Once you learn to see the story-line, you can't unlearn it. It will always be with you. And this is the sweet spot you'll need to truly step into the role of CEO in your life.

So, take a minute to do a deep dive into your money picture and tease out what your numbers are telling you. Look at the data you've been collecting and ask yourself these questions:

1. What do you notice when you look at what you have of value and what you owe other people (your assets and liabilities)?

2. What jumps out at you when you review what you're bringing in and what you're spending (your income and expenses)?

3. What are your numbers telling you?

You might be surprised to learn that you're better off than you thought. You might see that you're carrying more debt than you're comfortable with. Perhaps it becomes glaringly obvious that you're not paying yourself enough. Your numbers will tell you where you need to make changes, if you take the time to listen.

## The Debt Question

Okay, let's talk about the thing we're all conflicted about ... *debt*! Oh, the debt question.... If you've achieved a six-figure income or beyond, chances are good you've played around with debt to get there. It might be in the form of credit card balances that you haven't managed to pay down, or a personal loan from a friend or family member. Maybe you found start-up funding assistance. Whatever your circumstances, carrying debt is a normal part of business but it can also create a lot of stress, realized or not.

There are two main sides of the debt coin and we all have an affinity for one or the other, in our business and our personal lives. Many of us are risk (read "debt") averse and do our darnedest to stay out of it at all costs. This type of entrepreneur will drive their top line to have cash on hand to pay for a new piece of equipment or educational training. They use credit cards and other debt vehicles but are uncomfortable if they can't pay them off monthly and think long and hard before taking on more than they can handle financially.

Entrepreneurs on the other side of the debt coin see debt as a means to a pot of gold at the rainbow's end. They're comfortable carrying credit and are motivated by the possibilities they see in spending more than they have. They see everything in terms of *undefinable ROI*, which basically means, "I'll spend now in the hopes that I'll see real financial benefit somewhere down the road."

Each of these approaches to debt have pluses and minuses. The conservative, no-debt-at-all-costs approach is supremely fiscally responsible, but it can also limit our potential if we miss a critical growth opportunity because of our fear of going into debt. Alternately, the spend-and-hope-for-the-best model can put you in the right rooms at the right time but often leaves new entrepreneurs buried under mounting, unsustainable debt. In different ways, both scenarios can feel terrible as we strive to navigate our business growth.

So, how do we turn that around? By looking at how we *feel* about debt and using that to outline a strategy that works for us. Getting some clarity around where we stand (really looking at the full dollar amounts we owe other people) can make it easier to avoid "shiny object syndrome." Particularly when we're first gaining traction, it can be easy to overspend without revenue to support it. Then a new opportunity comes along that seems like the answer to our prayers, and we add another $3,000 to the nearly-maxed Visa. It feels good and bad all at the same time. If you're in this situation, where your debt is drowning you and you can't seem to stop spending, don't panic! There's a way to mend your broken financial fences.

When I work with clients, dealing with any debt they've taken on is a significant part of our conversation. If an entrepreneur has racked up credit card debt, but that spend isn't translating to additional revenue, it's time for a conversation. Most of us go into it feeling like a truant child, so do yourself a favor and take a deep breath. Remember that you made your spending decisions with the best of intentions and beating yourself up after-the-fact isn't going to solve the problem. What *will* help is doing a little basic math to put a plan in place.

Look at how much debt you're currently carrying. In an ideal world, we'd get you to the point where your use of credit cards or credit lines is simply to support your cash flow, and it's paid off every month. To get to that state of financial nirvana, we need to be hyper-vigilant and clear about our decisions. The equation goes like this: Whatever your debt total (let's say $10,000 for easy math), you'll need to generate that much in revenue plus 30 percent for the taxes on that income *just to pay off the debt*. This doesn't include any of your other overhead costs or having money on hand to pay yourself. How many new clients do you need to generate that amount? How much additional revenue will you need to maintain the business? And how many extra clients on top of that will you need to put some money in your own pocket?

It feels daunting, doesn't it? For a lot of entrepreneurs, the answer is simply to put their head down and keep on keeping on, hoping for the best. I'd like to suggest an alternative. Now that you're more familiar with the actual numbers in your business, look at how much extra is on hand that you could be putting toward your debt every month. Can you find $25, $100, or even $1,000 a month to put toward your debt load? What can you cut – or what new spending can you put off – that will allow you to make some progress in reducing your debt? Too often, people don't see the value of the small debt set-aside; it becomes an all-or-nothing self-fulfilling prophecy. "It's too much, what's the point? I'll just pay the minimums until that big kahuna client comes in and then I'll right the ship." The problem with this logic is that, by the time the big client comes in, there will be other needs in the business, and as we know, if we don't give our money a job to do, it will get spent elsewhere. So, I encourage you, if you're carrying uncomfortable debt, to confront it head on and plan to tackle it, one dollar at a time, until you get "over the hump" and your business can support your spending without paying extra finance charges every month.

Once you've accomplished that, map out future expenses based on which kind of entrepreneur you are – the saver or the spender – and hold yourself accountable in a way that feels great to you. If you tend to be uncomfortable with overspending and you find it's limiting your ability to grow using "good debt," break down a scenario where a little debt discomfort would be worth your while and how you would manage it, so when the opportunity arises you can say "yes" without fear. And if you tend to sign up without a plan for paying off debt, put checks and balances in place that force you to have a specific plan in place to put cash in the bank to cover the cost, so you can feel great about the new program or that new part-time hire. Knowledge is power and knowing your debt habits will go a long way toward alleviating any guilt, stress, or fear around it.

## The Shell Game

I have a client who has, by all accounts, built a spectacular business in a very short amount of time. She grew from literally nothing to multiple six-figures in less than six months using nothing but her gifts, grit, and determination to not fail. Many aspects of entrepreneurship have come easily but mastering the money game has taken a little longer. Despite booking high five-figure months, she always felt she was on the verge of disaster because she was playing the shell game.

In my view, the shell game is the worst place to be as an entrepreneur because it's the most uncomfortable. It's when there simply isn't enough money to go around, so you keep moving in fits and starts, all the while feeling like the other shoe is about to drop and you'll be shown up as the fraud your secret mind says you are (hello, *bear brain,* there you are again!).

For this client, the shell game felt very familiar. Having spent most of her life working very hard for little money, my client was intimately aware of all her bills, exactly how much she was making, and how to pay just enough to make everything work, but without getting ahead in any one place. She would get a little extra money and she'd treat her family to a nice dinner out. This would bring her back to the near-famine state around money she was most comfortable with.

These habits followed her to her new business. Despite keeping her initial expenses low, she was still constantly playing the shell game for two reasons: Her booked numbers were great but the cash flow was still catching up, and she kept taking every penny out of the business, assuming she'd simply earn more the next week. And she did! I started working with her around the time she hit her first six figures, and I was blown away by her earning potential. But the "living on the edge" pattern kept repeating itself. The more money she made, the more she found to spend on, and the more she needed to live on in her personal life. She had created in her business the exact scenario around money she'd known all her life, just with bigger numbers.

It's taken a while, but today this client has a different view of sufficiency and has changed her habits around money. Now she has a cash buffer built up in her business accounts and we implemented automatic transfers so that 30 percent of every dollar that comes in is set aside for taxes, so she's never caught short (one stressor alleviated!). She has developed a personal spending plan that feels good and allows for fun *and* long-term goals at the same time. Most importantly, she's not spending energy mentally and physically moving money around all the time. Just that has changed her outlook on her finances and her sense of well-being tremendously.

## Bear Brain: I Can't Actually Achieve All That!

The thing that's going to come up as you get more and more clear around your financial whys and wherefores is that little voice telling you it's just not possible. If you've developed a plan to get out of debt, I can guarantee that *bear brain* is going to try to get you to sink back into old habits at some point. The questions of "What's the point?" will crop up, you'll lose sight of your goals, and your clarity will go into the toilet. But that's only a problem if you let it become your long-term story. We all have doubts, particularly when we've set ourselves giant financial goals. If we're not completely comfortable managing our money, it's no wonder that doubt and self-sabotage will creep in along the way.

What do we do about it? Refocus on our goals, step back, and take that bird's eye view of our situation to put *bear brain* in its place. You *can* achieve a blissful financial reality. It likely won't happen all at once; silver bullets aren't standard issue in the entrepreneurial world. But if you can maintain your clarity of purpose – do the right things, for the right reasons – you can thrive. Tell that to your *bear brain* when it tries to tell you to play small around your money decisions!

## REFLECTION QUESTIONS

1. Who are you making this change in your finances for? How does it feel?

2. Are you listening to your money story? What is it telling you?

3. What relationship do you have with debt and how can you use that to your advantage?

4. How can you continue to feel in control with your finances?

---

## EXERCISE
# Your Path to Empowerment

This purpose of this exercise is to look back over the work you've done so far and reflect on what's changed in your relationship with your finances. Consider the following questions and write down your answers so you can come back and review them as often as you need:

1. What is going well and what feels better when you look at your *Zen Money Map?*

2. What's feeling difficult now that you have a full view of your financial picture?

3. If things are still feeling "ick," where do you think it's coming from and what would alleviate it?

4. How has this work changed your view of money?

5. Are you feeling more in control or less? Why do you think that is?

6. On a scale of 1-5 (1=low, 5=high), how empowered do you feel today with your money management?

—————— **EXERCISE** ——————
# Abundance Meditation

As I'm sure you've experienced, digging into our numbers can cause a great deal of discomfort. Finding that beautiful result of *feeling* good around the actual money management can be elusive, particularly when we're nervous around the whole subject in the first place. A good friend of mine who works with creative professionals gave me this simple meditation to share with you. She started using it years ago when she was stressed about money. She knew being in that "stressed state of mind" would scare opportunities away, so she created this meditation to work herself out of that state of desperation, intentionally combining growth (greenery), money, flow (water), and happiness. I like it because it's simple and requires just a few minutes of your time. You can do it when you are waiting for the bus or stuck in a line at the bank to release on any negative beliefs around money and invite in abundant thinking.

Close your eyes (if it's safe to do so, otherwise create a mid-distance "soft gaze") and imagine you're in a serene place where you are surrounded by lush greens, perhaps a field with tall grasses, a pine forest, or a thick jungle. You can smell moist soil and the sprouting, young green leaves. Envision yourself sitting or standing near a brook, creek, or river, as you hear the flowing water gurgle and birds singing in the background. Take slow, deep breaths. When you look at the running water, you can see money floating down the stream. Say to yourself, "Let it flow." When you're feeling calm and content, look up. You're surrounded by people you care about, smiling, happy, and relaxed. Let yourself to be immersed in this calm, beautiful environment for a few minutes.

This meditation allows us to center ourselves around money. Do this whenever you're feeling off-balance as you continue to develop your relationships with your finances and establish sound habits. It will allow you to feel more connected with your choices and free your mind from *bear brain* to allow you to see ways you can take further advantage of your money, both in your business and your personal life. It can be very liberating, particularly as part of your on-going financial rituals.

## Bottom Line

It takes effort – the Right Effort – to maintain our financial integrity. That doesn't mean it has to be hard, however. Standing firmly in the rituals you've created, listening to the story your money is telling you, and being wildly curious about how you handle increased revenue as well as debt is a fantastic way to keep moving forward on your journey to *Zen Money*. Pairing your new-found view of your finances with meditation or other spiritual rituals can further help you along your path to the Middle Way.

You've established good habits, have opened yourself up to delving further into your financial situation (even if it's a little

## Chapter 8

# The Right Mindfulness and the Right Concentration

*"You are not here merely to make a living. You are here in order to enable the world to live more amply, with a greater vision, with a finer spirit of hope and achievement. You are here to enrich the world, and you impoverish yourself if you forget that errand."*

**~ Woodrow Wilson**

We've come so far! The last two tenets of the Eight-Fold Path are the Right Mindfulness and the Right Concentration and we're going to dive into them now. These two stops along our *Zen* path are often discussed in tandem because they're so closely related. In a nutshell, having the right mindfulness means being aware of your actions, words, and thoughts. Most people agree that our thoughts, speech, and deeds have power, and to stand in integrity, we must be hyper-aware of how we use them. It is just as true of our relationships with money, since what we imagine often comes to be.

In parallel, with the right concentration, focusing on and remaining fixed to a single object or goal can create expansive balance in our lives. In this context, I define that as striving with a single purpose to achieve our financial dreams. Let's take a look at how you can further enhance your money management with these two tenets.

## Training Your Brain

Much of what we've covered so far has been with the goal of training (or retraining) your brain around money. To continue that process, we need to be very aware of how we make decisions around our finances, and what happens if we change our habits. Is it easier to consider charging more for your services, or to put off making that purchase to keep your finances in line, now that you've put some new habits in place? If you've noticed your inner dialogue around money shifting, you're actively engaged in retraining your mind. Congratulations!

The primary way to continue this work is to stay on track with the financial rituals you've established and continue to monitor your thoughts, feelings, and actions when it comes to money. My guess is that as you continue to stretch and grow in this area, you'll see starts and stops along the way. That's okay! The important thing is to keep at it until knowing your numbers is as natural as breathing.

## Your Big Vision

At the beginning of the book, I asked you to think about your *big why*, the reason you're working so hard in your business. Many of us are interested in more than just growth for growth's sake, and if you're anything like my clients, you not only want to build a business of value, but you want to live well and ultimately help as many people as you can. This is the core of your *big vision*. And for us to be able to make it all happen, we need to have a handle on how it all works together to fund our wildest dreams.

Whether you call yourself a soul-preneur, or a spiritual entrepreneur, or are just someone who has a vision for massive change in the world, I'm guessing you have a great version of a *big vision*. Perhaps you ultimately want to help the homeless in your city and you're building a business to help you fund that. Maybe you see a world where no child is hungry – ever – and you are using your genius to make that happen. Maybe it's simply to send your kids to college and help your husband retire from the job he detests, to feel completely free and unencumbered in your life. Many of us are familiar with the concept of "start with why." But I want to ask you to flip that idea on its head.

I was in a room of rock star entrepreneurs a while ago and one of the speakers shared something that made a lot of sense to me. He said, "The first step is to build a solid financial base. Once you're not tied to the day-to-day, when you can get up when you want to get up and do what you want every day, *then* you can find your *why* and create huge impacts in the world." It stuck with me because he distilled what I've been attempting to teach down to two sentences. Why is it so important? Because we can't fund our movements from a leaky financial ship. And we can't dream *really big* when we're stressed about our money situation.

So, do me a favor and consider where you are on your world-changing trajectory. Is your financial house built on a solid-enough foundation to fund your daily personal dreams? At what point will you have enough cash to start funding your *big vision*, too? Part of the beauty of developing a relationship with our money that's tied to our mission, is that it forces us to look at the nitty-gritty money stuff with a new purpose. Not just to pay bills and stay on the entrepreneurial treadmill, but to use our financial decisions – all of them – toward that ultimate purpose. And step one is getting right with the numbers in your business and your personal life. Then, when you're feeling ridiculously abundant, it's so much easier to think bigger than ever, and to fund your *big why*.

## Funding Your Wildest Dreams

The choices you make in your business ultimately flow down to how much money you're able to take home as reward for your hard work. Like all the other equations I've asked you to consider, it all comes down to simple math and we can work it backward to give you a concrete plan. Think of your current *big vision*. How much money would you love to commit to it, above and beyond your business and personal financial needs? Let's start with $100,000 just for fun (I'm sure you'll want to be able to put more than that to your mission in the long run). And let's say that to live in a state of abundance in your personal life, you need $10,000/month in your pocket. (This is debatable, as studies have shown that earnings over $75,000/year do *not* necessarily equate to increased happiness, but again, for ease of numbers, we'll use $120,000 cash in pocket.) How much do you need to generate in your business for that to work? Well, it depends. (I know, you hate that I keep saying that, but it *really does*!) Let's say you run a lean and mean model and your average expenses are $5,000/month, or $60,000/year, and we want to set aside 30 percent for taxes on top of all of that. Our business needs to bring in $257,000 in a year just to cover your business and personal life. This is cash in hand, remember, not contracts that haven't yet been paid or possible write-offs when people fail to pay us. If we want to add another $100,000 of *big vision* spending to that, we need to generate $400,000. ($400,000 revenue - $120,000 taxes - $60,000 = $220,000 ($120,000 for you and $100,000 for your big mission.)

Seems like a lot, doesn't it? And it doesn't include additional expenses you likely will need to pay to generate the additional income (extra travel, additional staff, etc.), nor does it consider any lifestyle choices you may feel necessary (hiring a stylist, new wardrobe, getting help to keep the house running while you're working hard in your business).

This example shows that while having the intention for creating massive change is wonderful, it's not enough by itself. Hence, our conversation about building your financial foundation *before* you can really drill down on your *big vision*. When I'm strategizing with my clients, we're always looking at our current money situation with an eye toward the long-game, but most of our focus is on the short-term goals. We can't get to the first, without being clear on the second. I want that clarity for you, too!

Consider how to build up to your vision and write down your plan. For one of my clients, getting her business ship in order included building a financial buffer of six months of expenses, and when we reached that, we targeted building up $20,000 cash buffer in several personal accounts as a cushion (paying down mortgage debt, continuing to fund her retirement accounts, and having a travel fund were part of that puzzle as well). Only when those major hurdles were crossed, did we begin setting aside cash for her *big vision* of helping local charities as a major donor. She could comfortably see herself stepping into that newer version of herself on a larger stage because her business was well-cared for and her personal finances were on track. It gave her incredible confidence to continue growing so she could give back at the level she desires.

What are your stepping stones to funding your wildest dreams? When do you want to achieve them and how will it feel when you start crossing milestones off your list? If you're anything like the amazing entrepreneurs I know, it'll feel pretty darn spectacular.

## Building Your Strategy

Remember the final piece of the *Zen Money* puzzle, the Right Concentration? Maintaining a clear focus on our big goal will help in building *and* achieving your *big vision*. The strategy you use should mirror what you've learned about yourself when it comes to money. If you're relatively risk averse, it's probably best to establish a strategy that allows for you to mitigate it, even if that means not growing as quickly as you may like. Alternatively, if you're more tolerant of carrying debt or have deeper resources to play with, your strategy may be able to include some aggressive financial goals. The key is to know yourself and pay attention to what *feels* good to you, not just what someone may be telling you is the right next move.

An example of this is a client who is always playing one step ahead of what she can comfortably afford, both in her business and in her personal life. As a successful spiritual entrepreneur, she often takes on expenses before a more conservative person might advise. This has looked like hiring before she was ready, paying to get herself in a room of influencers without having many resources to back it up, and generally living more hand-to-mouth than might be comfortable for others. Some months she can't take as much out of her business as she'd like, and her cash flow is somewhat sporadic. However, it works for her. Why? Because she's the kind of person who thrives in financial adversity, and she's comfortable with some fluctuation around her income. If she *needs* to make the sales happen because she's taken on more than she can afford, she rises to the challenge every single time. She knows that if she wants to achieve her big goals, she needs to keep pushing herself in this way.

For other people, this strategy would be completely debilitating. I have another client who prefers a calmer, more levelled approach to growth. This copywriter has a very systematic formula for determining when it's time to invest in a new opportunity (she has the money in the bank to afford it), and she approaches her business development the same way. Her workflow allows her to take on a very specific number of clients each month, she takes home a very consistent income, and she plans out months in advance. This feels amazing for her, because financial certainty in her business is so important.

It allows her to pay herself consistently, and work toward her big goals over time.

These approaches couldn't be more different, but the feeling of calm and security around their financial decisions is identical. There are thousands of versions of *Zen Money* – we just need to identify what feels best for *you*.

## Drawing Your Treasure Map

It's time to draw your treasure map! What does that mean? Well, I'll be honest … we're going to talk about the "b" word. Yep, budgeting. I talk more in-depth about this important financial process in *From Zero to Zen*, but I want to touch on it again, because it's an area where many people completely shut down. We know we're supposed to have one, but we don't really know how to use it. Maybe you spend a lot of time putting a budget in place, only to stick it in a drawer. Regardless of where you are in your personal life or your business, budgeting is a standard tool we need to talk about, because from a financial management standpoint, it's a great road map.

A budget is a great planning and dreaming tool and we can use it to put all the different pieces that we've covered in one place. A true budget starts by looking at what happened historically, and then we build a projection based on that. So, let's talk a little about what the budgeting process really looks like. I like to think of it as a Google map for your business. It can actually be a really fun process. Imagine you're sitting in your car, ready to head out onto the road. A budget can help you get out of the driveway; it can help you know if there's an awesome coffee shop on the corner; or decide whether to take the winding little road or the fast highway. A budget can help us make all those decisions and have a much clearer picture of where we can go financially.

You can call it a spending plan if that makes it easier to ponder. Basically, since most of financial management is a backward look (what did we do last month, last year?), this is the place where we can dream and scheme for the future. All you have to do is review your financial information and consider what might be changing in your income and expenses for the next year. Once you have a story that feels great to you (based on your understanding in this moment), you have a road map for your business or personal life. Simple, right? It certainly can be. So why is it so hard to maintain?

I had a client once who was so resistant about the "b" word that we could barely get through a call. She freely admitted just hearing it made her want to completely shut down. She felt it was inappropriately restrictive. I've had clients tell me that they simply can't get behind a budget because it cramps their style. Mostly I hear this from entrepreneurs who aren't very familiar with what's happening in their businesses and are afraid to look. The budget becomes a lightning rod for that underlying discomfort. My response is to ask them how they know it's cramping their style if they're not actually sure what's going on with their money? I'd ask you the same if you're avoiding the "b" word, too. With this particular client, when we reframed the definition to "road map" for her business, we could finally take a deep breath and have a positive conversation around using a budget. She was no longer trapped by the concept once I assured her that it didn't mean success or failure in, and of, itself.

Here's what I want you to keep in mind about developing a budget or spending plan: It's just one tool in your financial tool box. It can help you determine if you're still on track for your big goals. That's it and that's all. There's no condemnation from a budget – that's completely self-inflicted if you're feeling it. So, ask yourself if you can let go of your anti-budgeting stories long enough to see its benefit as a tracking tool. It's one of the easiest ways for you to level-up your CEO game. Give it a try … I dare you!

## Bear Brain: I've Got This … Time for Something New!

Wondering where *bear brain* will show up as you move into these final stages of mapping your *Zen Money* life? Time and again, I've seen it rear its head as our ego telling us we're all set, that it's okay to set this hard work down and move on to something more fun and exciting. When that urge to say, "Screw it, we're done here," pops up, be prepared to go straight back to the good practices you developed in Chapter Six, and review where you stand on a regular basis, so that your know-it-all *bear brain* falls back into a deep hibernation where it belongs.

Having trouble staying on track? If you find yourself regularly tipping away from your middle path of financial health, bring yourself back by honoring your weekly review of your business and personal finances. Track yourself against your big goals and celebrate your achievements so far. Share your wins as well as your losses with a trusted friend or partner, to help keep yourself accountable to your financial work. Making it exciting and fun is the best way I know to combat it.

## REFLECTION QUESTIONS

1. How does your current financial flow make you feel and how can you tweak it to better meet your business and personal needs?

2. How will you continue to train your brain around your finances?

3. What is your overall money strategy and how will it help you achieve your goals?

---
### EXERCISE
---

## Map Your Financial Flow

This exercise will help you clarify how best to manage the ins and outs of your cash flow. You can look at your business and your personal life; you'll likely see trends when you compare things side by side. Here's what I'd like you to do:

1. Review your bank and credit card statements for the past two months and identify where and how much money you spent. List all your purchases for those eight weeks. You'll start to see a pattern in your expenses. When does your phone bill come due? What about your credit card? How much did you spend on "miscellaneous items" and what exactly were they? Asking yourself these types of questions will help you drill down on what you're spending and analyze whether it's

helping you achieve your goals on your way to your *big vision*.

2. Pay attention to your timing. Did you pay anything late? One way to make sure you're paying your bills on time is to review your expenses every week. Enter any bills and check to see if they need to be paid immediately or if you have a grace period. Even taking ten minutes every Friday to check on your bills can ensure you never pay a late fee again. Setting up autopay is a lovely option, but it also tends to make us complacent, so check in now and again on the dollars going in and out of your accounts so you can stay on track.

3. Review your activities and record keeping. Are there ways to streamline your work so it doesn't take as much of your time? Developing a plan for your bill paying that mirrors your income flow is a great way to manage your money and leave you feeling in control and confident.

## EXERCISE
# Dream a Dream

Let's set your new money vision down on paper! Getting really clear on our financial goals and then stating them to the universe is an exceptionally powerful exercise. Now that you have a much better handle on your numbers and how/where you want to go with your business, please take some time this week to dream up your big picture. These questions will help you get started:

1. What's your money vision now and has it changed at all? Is your *big why* the same or has it expanded?

2. Explain your new money management plan. Who is doing the bookkeeping/record-keeping work? How often? What tools will you use to stay on track?

3. How will you feel about the money in your life and how can you stay on track with abundance?

4. Are you feeling 100 percent confident yet or do you need additional help to get there? What might that look like?

Once you've answered these questions, you can take a stab at setting a spending plan for yourself in both your business *and* your personal life. Here's how you do it: Take the past twelve months of income and expenses (spreadsheet is a great way to look at this, but you can write it out long-hand too if that's easier for you). Add a budget column. What do you think the next twelve months will look like, in terms of costs and income? Ballparking those numbers, based on where you've been recently, is a great starting point.

Then add in any additional expenditures or income sources you see coming down the road. Take a step back and consider the whole picture your new budget is showing you. Is the story one you like? If not, where can you add and cut to make it your dream come true? A tool like this can give you added depth to your business planning, and ultimately to your ability to achieve your big goals.

## Bottom Line

Maintaining your focus on your thoughts and actions around money is the name of the game. As we get more and more comfortable with how money comes in and out of our lives, it can be easy to stop short, to not fully commit to our ultimate dreams. Staying on track by looking at your numbers regularly, using tools like a budget, and staying true to your long-term financial goals for your business and your personal life can help you bring your *big vision* to life.

Along the way, we don't want to lost sight of our feelings around all this new information. If you're finding yourself getting tense, or wanting to stop reading, sit quietly and take a series of deep breaths. Remember why you picked up this book in the first place. This discomfort is normal, and while it may be intense, it is certainly better than carrying financial fear around for the rest of your life. Be kind to yourself as you become more competent navigating your numbers and remember that no one is born knowing all of this. It takes time to fully step into your shoes as a savvy, confident CEO.

And when you step up your money game in this way, you're that much closer to finding your version of *Zen Money*. All that's left is bringing it all together in a perfect balance … that's just right for *you*!

## Chapter 9

# The Middle Way

*"We make a living by what we get. We make a life by what we give."*

**~ Winston Churchill**

You've done it! We've walked our *Zen Money* path through the eight tenets of the Right Understanding, the Right Thought, the Right Speech, the Right Action, the Right Livelihood, the Right Effort, the Right Mindfulness, and the Right Concentration. It's now time to consider your Middle Way, how you'll incorporate all of these into your new financial reality and stand fully in your financial *Zen* with ease.

To me, the Middle Way is about finding your balance. Traditionally, it referenced a path of moderation – which we have termed beautiful sufficiency – between the extremes of self-indulgence and self-sacrifice. You're now seeing the benefits of approaching your money management through this lens. It's the best feeling in the world to know exactly why you're making a financial choice, and to have a plan for your money that helps your business grow, allows you to thrive in your personal life, *and* gives you a platform to achieve great things in this world. That knowing is completely possible if we walk this middle path, where sufficiency is the name of the game, but we are still allowed to indulge ourselves occasionally, secure in the knowledge that we're standing on a firm financial foundation.

The reality is that there are hundreds of ways to achieve an equilibrium with your finances. And there are thousands of ways to feel great about your money. Your version of *Zen Money* is going to look different than mine or any other entrepreneur. The important thing to remember is that how you build it is entirely up to you. Now that you have some solid ideas on how to put your money to best use for *your* business and in *your* life, I hope you can begin to see what your version of financial balance may look like.

## Law of Resources: Finding Your Sufficiency

The main take-away from this book, if you gain nothing else, is that you – and only you – are responsible for how you use your resources. In the entrepreneurial game, it's easy to believe that our opportunities are endless and that we will enjoy all the success we desire. Let's believe in that whole-heartedly. I'd also like you to build that dream in a fiscally responsible way.

That means having a plan for the money that's coming into your business, and recognizing that in any given moment, it's a finite amount. If you choose to use up all your financial resources within your growing business, you will have nothing left for yourself. You may find yourself undermining your efforts by taking out more money than your business can afford. Or you may attempt to reinvest so heavily that you create uncomfortable money problems in your personal life or in your relationships. None of these scenarios allow you to achieve your biggest desires and wildest dreams of giving back to your community and living the life you're striving so hard to create.

Many of my clients have created a beautiful relationship with money, by going through these practices and putting a few simple financial rituals in place for their businesses. One client finally silenced her *bear brain* which told her she couldn't possibly charge more, and increased her pricing after nearly two decades in business, to huge success. Others have stopped worrying about making their mortgage payments because they know exactly where their money is coming from and how to use it. Using the exercises and meditation practices, they're now confident in their money management in their businesses, know exactly how much they can pay themselves (with plans to increase that regularly), are working on paying down debt, and their ease – and excitement – around money is apparent every time we talk. That's my definition of beautiful sufficiency in a nutshell!

So, I encourage you to find *your* version of sufficiency. That financial flow – with its middle-way approach to money management – will allow you to look at what's happening with your money in a new way. You'll be able to make informed decisions about how you grow the best version of your business, while establishing the lifestyle you want and creating the change you crave. The good news is that your definition of sufficiency will shift over time, sometimes even week by week, as you achieve higher and higher levels of success as an entrepreneur. By continuing to apply the tenets outlined here, you'll not only grow an amazing business, but your sense of satisfaction will be infinitely greater because it's grounded in you being completely clear on *why* and *how* you're using your money to your best advantage.

## Enjoying Financial Flow

A question comes up often when I'm talking with entrepreneurs who've started seeing major traction in their businesses: What do I need to be doing with my finances? It's a great question, and you're going to hate my answer (hint: it's familiar): It depends, on you, your goals, and your particular circumstances. But since that's not entirely satisfying, I'd like to offer some additional observations.

There are three main types of business owners when it comes to financial management. And often, which type you are has a parallel to your personal life as well. We can learn to shift and change as we continue to learn and grow, but we all have tendencies when it comes to how we'd prefer to deal with our finances. The main financial types are as follows:

1. The Architect: This entrepreneur is comfortable managing the daily record-keeping for her business and may even take care of her own taxes. She isn't daunted by the ins and outs of bookkeeping; in fact, she may even enjoy the work. This type of entrepreneur is fully confident managing all the tasks for her financial house and may go a long time before feeling

the need to hire additional help around her finances, to take over daily bookkeeping duties or for higher-level strategic support. She likely takes good care of her own personal finances and may manage her own investments without an advisor.

2. The Baker: This type of entrepreneur knows what needs to happen generally and may have a bookkeeper she calls on once a month (or once a year) to create her financial reports, most likely for tax purposes but possibly also for management review and decision-making. She is comfortable making spending decisions and knows where her money stands but enjoys having someone she trusts providing additional assistance in her financial kitchen throughout the year. She may have an advisor to assist her in building her personal nest egg.

3. The Celebrity: This entrepreneur knows that money management is not her zone of genius and delegates the day-to-day financial work as soon as possible for her business. She's likely to work with a financial partner or CFO who can help her identify opportunities within her business as well as coordinate taxes and other reporting requirements. She likely appreciates working with personal financial advisors who understand the entrepreneurial mindset and builds her team to support her *big vision* early on.

4. The Dancer: This entrepreneur wants to make a difference in the world but looking at her numbers leaves her feeling uncomfortable to say the least! She spends quite a bit of time avoiding her money

management and consistently carries anxiety about her financial circumstances. She's likely to continue dancing away from this part of her business until the discomfort becomes too much to take and she begins to shift into becoming one of the other archetypes. She usually doesn't work with anyone in particular for her business or personal finances but may utilize someone for tax coordination (which is kept at arm's length and only when necessary).

5. The Editor: This final archetype is an "entrepreneur's entrepreneur", someone who knows exactly what needs to happen with her financial management. She's taken care of it all in the past (and may previously have identified as the Architect) but is ready to delegate this piece of her business to a trusted advisor. She recognizes that to grow her business, she needs someone dedicated to her financial growth at her side moving forward. The Editor appreciates working with smart, qualified people who will get things done and help her achieve her big goals.

While the financial flow between business, personal, and giving back is the same for these three types, each of them enjoys their *Zen Money* differently. These examples can help you consider how you want to manage your money going forward and potentially what kind of help you may enjoy as your grow your business. To take a deeper dive into exactly what type of entrepreneur *you* are, and additional insights for building your *Zen Money* strategy, take the Financial Archetype Quiz at www.zenmoneymap.com/financialarchetype to learn more.

# Dealing with Setbacks

We're all set and ready to go with our new financial know-how and plans! Except … what happens when we fall off the wagon or get buried in client work? Setbacks are inevitable as you create your *Zen Money Map*. Let's explore some of the ways things might derail for you and how to get back on track.

## The Best Laid Plans

You've been actively practicing your financial rituals and it's feeling great! You're starting to see how the money is flowing in your life. And then you get sick, or need to travel for a month, or simply feel exhausted and can't keep up with your weekly money date. You might start to worry, as your newfound comfort around your numbers starts slipping away.

Don't panic! You can get back on track just as easily as you boarded the *Zen Money* train in the first place. Just pick up where you left off and recommit to the work. A slip will likely further invigorate your resolve around managing your money, now that you know how great it can feel. Just don't beat yourself up about it in the process. Remember: Money is just a tool, and it's not judging you one way or the other.

## The Pendulum Swing

You may find that when one area of your financial life is going well, another area becomes a problem. The business is thriving, and you're managing your growth like a pro. You're even paying yourself a decent wage. And then your boiler goes on the fritz just after you booked that vacation you've been planning for with your husband. All of a sudden, the urge to use your business as a cash drawer hits you hard.

Don't panic! You know in your gut the solution to this problem. And if you determine that the only way to keep the roof from caving in over in your personal finances is to take out additional equity from the business, that's totally acceptable – *as long as you understand the consequences of that decision.* You may have to put some of your business goals on hold or take less pay next month. Perhaps there's another resource outside of your business you might choose to utilize instead. At the end of the day, if you're looking at your full financial picture alongside your big goals, a temporary setback can be easily overcome. It's when we keep striving for "business as usual" while dealing with unexpected expenses, that we put ourselves in financial jeopardy.

## Going It Alone

This book has been entirely about how to empower yourself as an entrepreneur and step fully into your role of CEO of your life. Too often, I've seen smart business people want to focus entirely on sales and marketing, and hope and pray the cash will follow, without fully understanding that knowing your numbers is the first step in creating a booming business. So, I love it when the entrepreneurs I know become familiar with basic financial concepts and start taking their money management to the next level. I love it because I see how *good* they feel with their new clarity and confidence in how they can use their money to their advantage. However, one pitfall I also see happening regularly is when entrepreneurs don't get help soon enough. It's easy to focus on getting help in other areas before your finances, but it can lead to unsustainable debt and feeling out of control.

Don't panic! There are plenty of qualified professionals out there to help you keep your financial house in order and offer experienced advice as you grow your business. Your version of this may look like hiring a bookkeeper, or beginning to work with a tax accountant, or bringing on a part-time CFO to help you look at your big picture around money. Wherever you're at right now, there is someone out there who can make your financial work easier and your flow better, so don't be afraid to reach out and ask for help. Asking for advice from trusted friends in the entrepreneurial world is a great place to start, as is taking the Financial Archetype Quiz to get started.

## Bear Brain: A Recap

I'm hoping that by now, you're familiar with how *bear brain* can show up for you in your business, your personal life, and specifically around your finances. And I'm *really* hoping it's clear that while it will raise its ugly head at the least provocation, it's also entirely possible to acknowledge that part of your mind that wants to keep you safe and appreciate its usefulness when there actually *is* a bear trying to eat your face, and then move on to do the things that will help your business – and therefore your life – thrive. Keeping an ever-vigilant eye out for the ways *bear brain* can crop up will help you stay on track with your money management and allow you to fully embrace your *Zen Money* reality. If it's possible for me, it's certainly possible for you!

## REFLECTION QUESTIONS

1. What does beautiful sufficiency mean to you? In your business? In your personal life?
2. What are your ultimate goals and what money strategy will allow you to achieve them?
3. Has your vision for your business, personal life, and big mission changed at all? If so, how?

---

### EXERCISE
## Your Ultimate Goals

What's your reward for all this hard work? Let's answer these questions and nail down your goals for getting yourself paid and funding your *big vision* while maintaining a sustainable business:

1. How do you plan on paying yourself and is it easy to maintain month after month?
2. What is your cash buffer number? How long will it take you to build it?
3. What is your financial cycle and who will ultimately be responsible for the day-to-day bookkeeping, the monthly reviews, and annual tax and reporting tasks?
4. How do you feel right now about your money management? How would you like to feel, and how can you achieve it?

## Bottom Line

The Middle Way for our *Zen Money* discussion includes finding that sweet spot between income and spending that feels abundant and allows you to grow your business according to your plans. It also allows you to pay yourself as part of your financial equation and develop a plan for the lifestyle of your dreams *and* your biggest mission.

Determining what type of entrepreneur you are around money is a great way to continue exploring what works best for you financially, in order to get the help you need or anticipate wanting in the future. Whatever your circumstances, there is a model that will work spectacularly well for you and knowing how to leverage it will help you create a business that thrives, live the life of your dream, and ultimately achieve your *big vision*.

Along the way, there will likely be setbacks. How you handle them will determine how successful you are. Considering what could derail you in your newfound *Zen Money*, so you're not caught short later, will help you ride the inevitable financial ups and downs much more smoothly.

## Chapter 10

# Your Bottom Line

*"Your vision will become clear only when you can look into your own heart. Who looks outside, dreams; who looks inside, awakes."*

**~ Carl Jung**

## Standing in Your Zen Money

Now that we've traveled together through the questions of *what*, *why*, and *how* of your finances, I hope you're able to see more clearly how nurturing your numbers in your business can translate to a windfall of not only cash in your pocket, but a true sense of confidence and ease in your life around money. Perhaps you've been able to redefine the concept of "beautiful sufficiency" for yourself and have started to apply it to grow your business, your life, and ultimately your view of the greater world.

To me, this is what standing in your *Zen* is all about. It's finding the connection between what wakes you up singing in the morning and sound financial management that will allow you to hit all the high notes in your song. If I could implant just one more thought in your head before we part, it's this: Enjoying *Zen Money* is as simple as paying attention to what you see and knowing that you already have everything you need to be successful at your fingertips.

All you have to do now is trust the process and stay in touch with your *why*.

## What Is Your Why Now?

Look back at the notes you took from way back in Chapter Two when you created financial goals in four categories (personal, relationships, business, community). Remember those? I want you to review them and see if anything needs to change, now that you have a deeper understanding of where you'd like to go (and how you can get there) financially. Is your *why* any different than when you first started reading this book?

If it is, and you've expanded your dreams, then take a clean piece of paper or start a new tab in your spreadsheet and answer the questions again with fresh eyes. This review is a great way to stay on track with our financial mission as we continue to grow and change as entrepreneurs. Inevitably as our view expands, our goals and our *why* do as well. Continual, meaningful reflection allows us to stay in touch with our long-term goals as we navigate our entrepreneurial adventure and all its ups and downs. Most of us know this inherently, and as entrepreneurs we're constantly re-evaluating to stay one step ahead. Our financial relationships deserve no less.

So, take a few minutes and ponder whether your *why* has changed in any way, or if you're simply more deeply committed to creating massive change in the world. That way, when you walk back into your everyday life, you'll take steps toward your *big vision* in every financial transaction you generate. Every drop of money in and out of your business, in and out of your personal checking account, can help move you toward those goals, your big *why*, and ultimately to following *your* version of the *Zen Money Map*.

## What's Next?

At this point, you should be feeling much more at ease in your financial worlds and know your next steps to growing a beautiful business, supporting your personal life, and working toward your goals. It should be clear how to build a strong bridge between your hard work and your pocketbook, in a way that *feels* good to you!

However, I know that's easy to say and not always so easy to accomplish, especially if you're flying solo. If you're wondering what the next steps might be, now that you're walking more comfortably in your money shoes, here are a few alternatives I see:

1. Take all you've learned and move on with your life, fall back into old money patterns, and put this book on a shelf until you're uncomfortable enough to reach for it again. Don't worry, the lessons will still be here for you.
2. Up-level your life by applying what you've learned to your business and your personal finances and continue building excellent financial relationships. Find out how

you can grow best by taking the *Financial Archetype Quiz*. Be a rock star with your money just as you are in every other area of your life.

3. Let me help you develop and implement a financial strategy that feels spectacular and works for *you*. Take advantage of my expertise to get your money in order so you can focus on doing what you love, knowing I've got your back. You can get started by visiting www.lizlajoie.com. Can't wait to hear from you!

## Find Your Zen

There will certainly be ups and downs as you learn to navigate your financial *Zen*. There will be setbacks and likely those old voices will try to redirect you back to that place of comfortable discomfort. Remember that you have tools to combat that now and can refer to them whenever you need. Tweak and change and start again, until your money management is consistent, and your rituals, habits, and general sense of financial well-being are second nature. Your business will thrive, your bridge will be solid, and your dreams will be within reach.

Thank you for joining me on this financial adventure. I wish you a great bottom line, a healthy and wealthy, beautifully sustainable life in all you do!

# Further Reading

*The Soul of Money* by Lynne Twist – A game-changer of a book that broaches the subject of "sufficiency" and encourages us all to redefine our relationships with money in ways that enrich our lives and those around us.

*The Big Leap* by Gay Hendricks – A must-read for all entrepreneurs that encourages you to see the ways you may be holding yourself back from true success, in all areas of your life.

*Start with Why* by Simon Sinek – An introduction to inspirational leadership that helps define our *big vision* and excite others to our cause.

*Sacred Success* by Barbara Stanny – An important read for anyone struggling to come to terms with money and the emotional responses that can keep you from finding true, heartfelt success.

*The Feel Rich Project* by Michael Kay – A wonderful introduction to personal financial management, with a focus on money mindset while developing a plan for your future.

## Acknowledgments

This book has percolated and coalesced alongside my work with incredibly talented and brave people, and is now in your hands, ready to make a difference. I'm grateful for everyone who shared their stories, thoughts, and practices, and helped me see this project into the world.

A heart-felt thank you to all the smart, creative, dedicated entrepreneurs I've had the pleasure of helping and learning from, along with those yet to come; you are at the center of this book. You've helped me craft my message through your stories, your successes (and failures that have become successes), and your willingness to dive into the sometimes murky and uncomfortable financial waters with me. It's a joy to work with you all.

I am forever grateful to Angela Lauria and everyone at The Author Incubator, who helped me birth not one but two books into the world, and who helped set me on my own *Zen Money* road in the process.

To the Morgan James Publishing team: Special thanks to David Hancock, CEO & Founder for believing in me and my message. To my Author Relations Manager, Gayle West, thanks for making the process seamless and easy. Many more thanks to everyone else, but especially Jim Howard, Bethany Marshall, and Nickcole Watkins.

To my beautiful family, who work so hard to keep me grounded while supporting my entrepreneurial dreams and meanderings along the way. I love you so!

And lastly, to my readers: thank you for sticking it through to the last. This book is for you, written with my highest hope that you find your path to *Zen Money*, one that allows you to achieve your wildest dreams … in a way that *feels* fantastic.

# About the Author

Liz Lajoie helps entrepreneurs master their finances and grow thriving businesses that support their passions and advance their big missions. She helps new and not-so-new entrepreneurs learn to step fully into the role of CEO and get the most out of their business. She specializes in specializes in a three-pronged financial approach that includes impactful business strategy,  integrated money management, and learning opportunities that meet clients wherever they are, helping them map a version of *Zen Money*™ that springboards growth and instills unexpected peace of mind. She understands how hard it can be to juggle the demands of entrepreneurship and knows having a financial guide on your side can make all the difference!

She helps her clients to let go of their financial fears, manage their money with an eye to the future, and become confident in their decision-making around money. She loves supporting entrepreneurs as they grow their businesses, helping find ways to increase profits while decreasing stress associated with their money management.

Liz has spent over fifteen years working with small business owners, honing her skills in financial management for entrepreneurs who "sell their brain" for a living. Along the way, she earned an MBA, learned exactly what it takes to be successful as an entrepreneur, and how to help people find their particular version of *Zen Money*. Liz's passion is helping online entrepreneurs fully enjoy the process of business building based on a strong financial foundation, one that supports their personal finances and their desire to give back. She lives with her family in northern New Hampshire.

**Website:** www.lizlajoie.com

**Email:** liz@lizlajoie.com

**Facebook:** www.facebook.com/zenmoneycfo

**LinkedIn:** www.linkedin/in/lizlajoie

## Thank You

I know how hard it can be to dig into your numbers and commit to doing the work outlined here. It can be an emotional roller-coaster, just as anything that causes us to stretch and grow. I hope that you feel it's been worthwhile, and that you're excited to take yourself, your business, and your big dreams to the next level along with your new understanding.

There are many ways to continue to have success with your finances, and to help you on your way, I've created your *Financial Archetype Quiz*. It's a great way to identify what kind of financial management will work best for you in your business and your personal life. Visit www.zenmoneymap.com/financialarchetype to take the quiz and start creating your *Zen Money Map*!

Morgan James makes all of our titles available
through the Library for All Charity Organization.

www.LibraryForAll.org